THE ROOTS OF DESIRE

THE ROOTS
OF DESIRE

*The Myth, Meaning, and Sexual
Power of Red Hair*

MARION ROACH

BLOOMSBURY

Published by Bloomsbury Publishing, New York and London
Distributed to the trade by Holtzbrinck Publishers

All papers used by Bloomsbury Publishing are natural, recyclable
products made from wood grown in well-managed forests.
The manufacturing processes conform to the environmental
regulations of the country of origin.

Library of Congress Cataloging-in-Publication Data

Roach, Marion.
The roots of desire : the myth, meaning, and sexual power of red hair /
Marion Roach.—1st U.S. ed.
p. cm.
Includes bibliographical references and index.
ISBN-10: 1-58234-344-6
ISBN-13 978-1-58234-344-0
1. Redheads. 2. Hair—Social aspects. 3. Hair—Erotic aspects. I. Title.

GT6735.R63 2005
391.5—dc22
2005040963

First U.S. Edition 2005

1 3 5 7 9 10 8 6 4 2

Typeset by Hewer Text Ltd, Edinburgh
Printed in the United States of America
by Quebecor World Fairfield

For Rex, simple as that

CONTENTS

Prologue

I WROTE THIS BOOK after a tale I was told turned lurid. Not lurid at the start; at first the story was of minor interest to me. At its beginning it was a simple rendering of scientific discovery, a relatively by-the-book identification of a genetic marker told to me during the time of the mapping of the whole human genome. The story seemed small, one of many such discoveries, and this particular genetic discovery did not appear to lead to cures or break-throughs, to serums, prizes, or fame—those being the usual standards required to pique a layperson's attention. And then there was the fact that in real time, the discovery was old news.

It was 1995 when a shy scientist in Edinburgh had discovered the gene for red hair. Following up on the work of others, he had advanced some pigmentary genetic research performed on mice and applied it to humans. And striking as red hair can be, what he had found was the clue to the hair color of fewer than 4 percent of the world's population.

Seven years passed before I read about the discovery. But when I did, I called Jonathan Rees, the man whose lab had done the investigative work on the gene. And even he seemed weary, his tone suggesting that there might be nothing more to say. Perhaps it had all been told, I suggested, politely making an effort to excuse myself from further interest. "No," he countered. Quite the opposite. Read the press he had gotten, he recommended, and see if anything pops out at you. It sounded like he had given this advice before. I wondered if his weariness resulted from that lead not being taken.

The armful of worldwide newspaper and magazine accounts of Rees's discovery are more soft porn than science. Tipped toward the seductive, inclined like the proverbial guys outside peep shows who beckon you inside, they are mottled with references to the highest-priced Roman female slaves, Vikings raping their way across the Northern Hemisphere, and erotic escapades of redheads from Eve to Rita. The stories were engorged with a sexual energy I had never seen before in plain tales of scientific discovery. And suddenly I was in love with the tale. But which tale? That of the science or that lustier one of the popular notions?

In 2002, the *Washington Post* ran a feature piece on redheads, mentioning Rees's work, pining, "Why do we want them so much now?" (insisting, thereby, that we do). The *Atlanta Journal-Constitution*, the *Cincinnati Enquirer*, and Gannett News Service offered features by writers who had colored their hair red in part to report on what they claimed was a huge surge in the worldwide purchase of the at-home coloring processes that delivered the hue—as well as the allure—of red hair. It was quickly followed by a United Kingdom news service piece stating that Scotland's redheads are more sexually attractive than redheads anywhere else in the world. That, I had to see.

In my research, I learned that in every culture of the world, in every recorded epoch, there was a strong reaction to those who carry the melanocortin receptor gene, known as MC1R, on their sixteenth chromosome. The pathology of beliefs we harbor as well as the totems of popular culture created about this hair color have struck every emotion in our hearts, from vehement terror to unthrottled lust, since the hue first appeared in humankind, some fifty thousand years ago.

Adam is said to have had a first wife who was a redhead, though Eve, wife number two, is also frequently depicted wearing nothing but her long red hair. Judas Iscariot is painted as a redhead, as is Mary Magdalene. In Greek mythology, redheads turn into vampires when they die. During the Spanish Inquisition, flame-colored hair was evidence enough that its wearer had nicked hell's fire and therefore had to be burned as a witch. An 1886 book by Augustin Galopin noted redheads as the strongest scented of all women. I learned that a person could be beaten "like a red-headed stepchild"; that, in 1912, phrenology revealed redheads make the best waitresses; that Hitler reportedly banned the intermarriage of redheads for fear of "deviant offspring"; that a Corsican proverb has you spit after passing a redhead; and that, in the words of an American political pollster, "You can't sell one on television. They look fickle."

Fickle? My mother used to call me fickle. She said it

traveled with my hair color. I prefer to think of myself as passionate and pursuits such as this book to be the spawn of curiosity. But I get red in the face with anger at "fickle." Hearing the word of the pollster shot me to that place of stored memory, that smudge of where we really come from, and out flew taunts of children on the playground, softened amid the register of phrases divulged in intimate and astonished passion or shouted by men on the street in various countries, most particularly my own—and they all were, in fact, about my color.

Something clicked in my mind when the tale was colorized from that of a genetic pigmentary marker to one of sex. It almost seemed like two separate stories. Or was it that the worldwide press had thought we wouldn't be interested in the scientific without these allusions to sexual? Was it possible that the erotic tidbits are in fact as much a part of the history of the world of red hair as, say, freckles?

What is on this gene, anyway?

I called back Jonathan Rees in Edinburgh. He suggested I read the criticism of the human genome project by James Watson, corecipient of the Nobel Prize for his discovery of the structure of DNA. In it, Watson suggests that those, like Rees, who are interested in the genome for reasons other than profit must button up their lab coats and go digging for the stuff they want because most other scientists won't bother. Little attention has been paid to the gene for pigments, whether it is for blond hair or black skin. And reading Watson's words reminded me that it had taken seven years for news of Rees's discovery to percolate up to me. Watson goes on to suggest that those sites on the genome that will bring fame and fortune will be explored and staked out with alacrity but that those sites that do not appear to harbor the potential for huge drug company profits, like the gene for red hair, will be around for a while before anyone understands them. How odd, I thought: how little we really know about what makes us the colors by which we identify another and ourselves. And how unfortunate, as well, since what that leaves us are mere biases and myths when responding to the colors we are. Reasonable thought has never prevailed on the topic of human coloration. Instead, we exist on stereotypes. And what are those based on? How did we arrive at those identifiers we have of the redhead as fiery, highly sexed, and emotionally unhousebroken?

I have been a redhead all my life. It's the first thing I mention when describing myself. It was how I identified myself when calling back Dr. Rees, offering the detail as some sort of chip of admission, a ticket to gain entrance to the story. There was no denying that it was also offered as a marker of my own deeply personal questions about identity.

The writer's pursuit of a story sometimes begins with a premise, a dare, an idea, a vengeance, perhaps. Sometimes, if you are very lucky or very uninformed, all you have is a very simple question. That was all I had.

How do we identify redheads? What are they, I wanted to know, and how did we come to think of them as we do?

What I couldn't have known is that spliced to that simple question was a tale that harbored Mendel as well as the darker side of Darwin, that rounded up sin (lots and lots of sin), eunuchs, sidekicks, trade shows, physiognomics, pregnant Midge dolls, painkillers, torqued metabolisms, mice, Michelangelo, the deep, indescribable scent of women, phenotypes, stereotypes, and, of course, witchcraft.

Which is where I'll start.

PART ONE

SINNERS

CHAPTER ONE

Wild, Oversexed Heathens, Banshees, and Queens

Redheaded Women and How
They Make Us Feel The Way We Do

THE EROTIC BAKER is plying her wares.

"Chocolate vulvas. I've got chocolate vulvas."

It is a modern witch who is comfortable advertising herself and what she's got to offer. And a brave one too. On a late-August Saturday at six P.M., holding hands while surrounding the baker stand eight dozen exhausted, cold, hungry witches who have driven, flown (in planes), and ridden the bus to cluster on a brazen Vermont hillside in the frigid air. And now they are being made to wait for dinner through a commercial break.

"Chocolate vulvas. I've got chocolate vulvas," the witch repeats, her massive hips swirling inside a crimped aqua skirt. She cantilevers up the hill, around a great walking stick, swizzling and gyrating with astonishing grace.

I am at witch camp. I was pulled here by the hair.

*   *   *

In his play *Bussy D'Ambois*, George Chapman blithely reminds the reader that to make the perfect poison one must include the fat of a red-haired man. Written in the late sixteenth century, the dialogue in which this reference occurs states that only flattery, so "like the plague," can strike the brain and rage in the entrails to a degree "worse than the poison of a red-hair'd man." This is tossed off as if it were common knowledge at the time—the very time the witch trials of Europe were raging and were soon to inflame Puritan America.

When I first read Chapman's quote, I was in my own snug library, safe at home, and it was merely an armchair idea to find a witch and ask her—or him—if red hair was still a component in the rituals of black magic. While the production of poison is not limited to witches, it seemed a more direct route—a safer one, as well—than interviewing a common poisoner. There was always the chance that the right witch would be versed in the dark arts and their recipes as well as in how the redhead was once an essential ingredient in poison. I had been meaning to find a witch, anyway. Having heard countless times that all redheads are witches, I knew that though it isn't true, it is part of what we think about when we think about red hair.

Simple enough. I added to the growing list of things I needed in order to report this book: a witch.

Finding one was oddly coincidental. Within days of adding it to my to-do list, I was riding north out of Manhattan on an Amtrak train when a bald, gold-earringed man in a business suit plunked down beside me. He looked no more like a witch than any other of the commuters did— his leather briefcase in one hand, a steaming cup of coffee in the other—but one thing led to quite another and before we were out of Yonkers he suggested that I get myself to witch camp.

"Witch camp?"

Who knew witches went to summer camp? Hell, who knew they rode the train to Albany? He smiled and said he was quite certain that at least some of my questions would be answered by his colleagues in Vermont.

What I was really beginning to ask about was the identity of redheads. Pondering Chapman's quote about the ingredients for poison, as well as its sixteenth-century date, I was not only wondering who they were when Chapman penned that line but also who they were before this time such that knowledge of their venomous power would seem so accepted. And I was looking for traces of that baneful identity in today's perceptions of red hair.

In the history of the world some themes loom large: Plate tectonics, religion, race, and language are several of the obvious ways to sort and tell. But alongside these, smaller themes exist. You could relate the history of the world through the topic of transportation, for instance; within that, perhaps, through sails. Sorting and shifting this way you might find something that tugs or stirs you by lighting up some old themes and connecting them for the first time. But to tell the tale as completely as you can requires that after seeing those first lights beckon as navigators, you go back and have another look at the world and its history, this time through the lens of that one theme.

To see the story of red hair requires sifting through history as a whole with a red lens. But it is a bifocal lens, split by as well as merged into our ideas about the color red and hair.

Red is the color of power. The word is derived from the

Latin *ruber* and *rufus* and the Greek *erythros*, which can still be seen in botanical use in the word *erythrogyne*, the red female part of a flower. Within the little word, but three letters in the English language, is carried references to blood and fire, which in themselves can be, respectively, life-giving or shed in violence, warming, illuminating, or used to engulf a heretic. Worn by Catholic cardinals, red signals their willingness to die in fight for their faith; worn by a soldier, the color makes an easy target but also covers any blood that is shed. Using only its varying shades, we can verbally run a vast range—vividly illustrating debt, for instance, by saying one is "in the red," or politics, by calling a person a "Red." Red, of course, is the color of anger, as in "seeing red," which is what we do when we lose control. Mars, the Red Planet, is named for the god of war. It is also the color of shame when we are "red-faced" and the color some of us attain after the unique suffusion of blood that conjoins the pleasure of orgasm.

The mere perception of red reportedly enhances the viewer's metabolism and increases both heart rate and respiration, which may be why it is used to signal the danger awaiting the viewer of the universally under-stood symbols of stop signs, stoplights, and, of course, lipstick.

For its own part, hair is integral to human semiotics, one of the signs and symbols we use to communicate who we are and one to which others respond when making decisions about just who we might be. Its dual purpose represents not only what we choose it to say about us—shaving our heads to a shocking baldness, say, or restraining hair in braids—but also what others perceive. Perhaps the weightier iden-tifier, in fact, is the latter: the cultural as well as personal history the onlooker brings to the observation. Want to know what your hair is saying to the viewer? The answer: Whatever it is they were taught to hear.

Hair represents the life force itself. Carried in lockets, encased under glass at the grave, burned in rites, saved in scrapbooks after baby's first haircut, it is something you may have of another that is tangible as well as singularly identifying. Inarguably more stirring than fingernail clippings, it is a palpable attachment to the beloved—or the hated. The Victorians wore four types of jewelry made from intricate workings of hair: mourning, commemorative, decorative, and sentimental. A letter is nice, a photo sublime, but consider "The Rape of the Lock," Alexander Pope's eighteenth-century poem, fueled, it is said, by the simple act of a man snipping some hair from a woman and the resulting feud between two families. There is something more at work with how we feel about the hair of another than the mere act of sentimental possession.

Together, the color and the corporeal matter of red hair make a flamboyant identifier that incites reaction. It has done so since the hair color's earliest portrayals in human storytelling. Not always pretty in its references, red hair has a power that is gorgeous to behold. But searching world history for legitimate mentions of red hair is another matter, requiring the researcher to look over the saga of humanity with a red filter, focusing an eye for attention paid to anyone or anything relating to this one rare trait. These moments are exceedingly few, but finding Chapman's quote reassured me that they are there. And, like my discovery of Chapman's play, I imagined that not only would other definitive statements about red hair be difficult to find but that they too would appear not so much as highway signs but rather as minute fingerposts, little guides throughout the vast history of the world.

But any such reference, I realized, must also be viewed both in context and over time. This presents its own challenges. Because while that little quote of Chapman might not seem like much, when looked at in the right light it burns bright, in this case, illuminated by the flames of the pyre on which so many witches were burned. At the time the quote was written, it was simply a recording of common knowledge and would not have aroused my sort of intense interest; it would have garnered a nod, not the gasp I gave it. In its time, the quote passed through the permeable place of opinion into simple acceptance without so much as a reflex gag. It was plain to all that it was the truth. But when read from a distance of time, the quote seemed to hold a truth that had a tale to be told.

That was the beauty of the vista I had on some of what I was looking for: these comments, occurrences, responses, and even trials and murders in the case of witches, would appear as part of a tale. That is, if I could find them.

While researching definitions and etymologies of *red* and its variegated shades, I was led to *lurid*, a word we now use to mean "gruesome," as in the details of a murder. First appearing in English in the early 1600s, it descended from *luridus* and carries in it an accurate way to describe something that is lighted or shining with a fiery glow—that is, wildly or garishly red. Something, perhaps, like a pyre. *Lurid* is listed in the thesaurus as an adjective depicting brownness, and it appears right after *foxy* and *livid-brown*, right before *auburn* and *Titian*. And in those few words, the red hair associations veer off in myriad directions: the cunning of the fox, the pooling of the blood that is the lividity of the dead, the flushing of blood to the face of the living and the passion associated with that response, the great artist who captured a Venetian fondness for red hair in his mysterious shades of paint.

And while the wordplay of those etymological roots lured me in, I couldn't read through history a single word at a time and then head out after each in search of flare-ups of the red hair experience. More on point would be to trace backward to their source aspects of beliefs about red hair that remain plain to many to this day. Because under scrutiny—under that red lens—what appears as plain as the hair on our heads may not be plain at all.

That redheads are untrustworthy, fiery, unstable, hot-tempered, highly sexed, rare creatures is what passes for common knowledge today. The belief that they are generally evil, deceitful liars, however, has nearly passed out of use. That they are witches is a belief that thrums through the inherited history of humankind, with lighter shades of it popping up here and there. But we have forgotten now that redheads were once handy to have in the pantry when planning to off someone, a notion that was once tossed back as easily as a bromide. Which means that while we have moved far in time, in our reaction to redheads we've only moved along the color wheel to warm from hot. While we no longer burn them at the stake, we still carry potent, inflammatory beliefs about their power. And some of those beliefs have ancient, perhaps even primitive, ancestors at their root.

What other fingerposts were left along the way and how far back would there be observable, identifiable evidence, totems of the beliefs about red hair? Along with being an ingredient for poison, redheads were rumored to possess powers of the occult. So the idea of witches performing rituals at summer camp held some real charm.

But only a particular kind of practitioner could cross into my line of inquiry, to reveal something of the history of the world of red hair. First, I needed to predominantly focus on witches who were white, because while both red hair and witchcraft exist worldwide, I needed to narrow the field of research to look at one belief—or one set of beliefs—at a time. There would be a tale to tell of the African American with red hair, for instance, but it would not be one of pagan worship. I suspected that natural red hair on people with black skin had its very own historic story that was more rooted in the horrors of slavery than in the practice of witchcraft.

The witches I needed would have to be heathens, Druid, or Wiccans—modern practitioners of what most of us call witchcraft, all of whom are part of a nature-based spirituality reported to be the fastest growing faith in the world: paganism. While it means different things to different people, paganism in its popular usage suggests pre-Christian, polytheistic, nature-based religions of the West. Originally, heathens were simply people who lived on the outskirts, or in the heath, and like most people who live out of town, they were late to new ideas—in this case, Christianity—and forever after suffered the sobriquet that later came to be associated with wild, sexually active godless folk. The word *pagan*, as well, originally meant nothing more—or less—than "hick."

Focusing in on pagan witch camps was easy. The Web is full of them, complete with online registration forms. Soon after reading through a few camp descriptions, I found the draw of experiencing something both current and ancient was too strong to resist. I signed up.

When researching how humans once worshipped and what they previously believed, we are usually confined to the solid world of the artifact, the icon, the shroud, and the relic. I wanted to see something live. And pre-Christian. Because while much of what is performed in contemporary organized religion comes via the laying on of hands across centuries, I knew that something older than the Christianity in which I was raised was what was needed here. Something organic and simple. Because though it is riddled with its own symbols, Christianity didn't single-handedly compose the vivid iconography it uses to illustrate its moral tales.

I wanted to apply the lens of red hair to how Judeo-Christianity often represents good and evil, the coolly virginal and its fiery alternate, assuming that both ideals are colorized versions, transposed and tinted from beliefs that came before. Imagining the evolution of the iconography as a colorization process, I wanted to see the "before," to catch a glimpse of how my beliefs had been shaded along the way. And in doing so, I learned that some of the things I believed about red hair were simply wrong.

For instance, going into this project I thought that the Irish were Celts and the Celts were red-haired. It's a common belief. Go into any Celtic store and witness the red-headed dolls and depictions; see the myriad red-haired Leprechauns on St. Patrick's Day. Further, I thought that red hair was derived from the Picts, a Celtic people whom the Romans described as fierce warriors and as having red hair. But much like reading about pagan religion in works by Christian scholars, we must discount the condemnation. In the case of the Picts' hair color, a Roman bias about red hair had long been in place by the time the Picts, who inhabited the northern and central highlands of what is now Scotland, were battling the Romans during the Roman occupation of Britain. The Celts as a whole—who wrote nothing down, perhaps considering it impious to do so— were similarly depicted by the scholars among their enemies. And we, in turn, have read those descriptions, which is how we have mistakenly come to identify both the Picts and the Celts as having red hair.

There are clues about the hair color of ancient people in the color hair they chose to give their gods. People tend to make their gods in their own image. The Thracians, for instance, a people in the central and southern Balkans who emerged as a distinctive culture during the third millennium B.C.E., fancied gods who had red hair and blue eyes, quite like the Thracians. Some Celts were redheads and so were some of those they worshipped, including the Morrigan, part of a terrifying triad of goddesses of war and fertility in whose names battle atrocities were committed. Inscribing for posterity a description of the aftermath of such a battle, Roman historian Dio Cassius describes the women on the losing side thus: "Their breasts were cut off and stuffed in their mouths, so that they seemed to be eating them, then their bodies were skewered lengthwise on sharp stakes." Such offering of heads is in line with the wartime price required by the Morrigan, who, despite being associated with the carrion crow, is depicted in many references as having streaming long red hair.

When the ancient Romans wrote about the Picts, they did so in a color that both explained and forgave the Romans' difficulty in conquering them: The Picts were recorded as being red-haired, and red as being the very color of Mars himself, the god of war. And while some of the Picts were red-haired—they were fair, certainly compared to the Romans—the depiction was in a color considered not only powerful but one the Romans also used in their dramatic comedies to distinguish the actors playing slaves, easily identifiable by their red wigs. In this, the color was associated with derision, allowing the Romans' red-haired designation of the Picts to make sense in its time and context but have little value in ours.

Some red-haired associations hold up under scrutiny better than others. Certain things *are* red, of course, like blood. But then there are those images whose redness seems to have been with us forever and whose history reveals that they are red in ways as complex and indigenous as language itself. For instance, my hope was that witch camp might provide me with a glimpse of the devil in his pre-Christian identity, the better to understand why centuries of representation have depicted him as red.

The idea of hell has been on the mind of humans in varying forms since our earliest thoughts. By the time of its first Christian representation, hell had been around for thousands of years, picking up imagery but retaining most of its pre-Christian meaning. The need for hell doesn't change much over time: humankind requires a balance to pure good, and so needs a version of where we go if we are cast from the goodness of this world and the next. My question was when in history the Old Poker became associated with the color red, and how his redness differs from the red with which we brush women of evil intent, the devil's handmaidens, his spawn: the witches.

And so I am surrounded by witches as the erotic baker hawks her chocolate vulvas, gyrating her way up the hill.

There are nearly two hundred people holding hands, mostly women—and perhaps fifteen men—and pretty much everyone is dressed in the tie-dye, Birkenstock, unkempt-hair, braless, hygiene-lite look known as "granola."

There are no lights, indoor toilets, or private showers at this particular encampment, no screens or doors on the massive bunk-style cabins scattered here and there along the rocky hillside. And then there's this little tiny issue about going "skyclad."

After I registered for witch camp, leaflets started coming in the mail listing needed provisions. I shopped for battery-powered lanterns, since there would be no electricity except at the dining hall, and heavy-weather sleeping bags, having been warned that it would be in the thirties at night. My brave friend Mary Elizabeth, who generously volunteered to go with me, whittled two wands and searched for robes with hoods. But despite our efficiency, we somehow missed the part about being skyclad.

And when it came up again in an e-mail, we were reassured that, in fact, not everyone in camp would be skyclad.

"Skyclad?" I typed back into the e-mail box.

Naked. Anywhere but the dining hall, I am told, where "being skyclad raises some real boundary issues for many people."

Mary Elizabeth's response was to remind me that it would make spotting the natural redheads easier.

It is wicked cold, even under the late summer sun. And for that reason, and others of our own, I am not naked and neither is Mary Elizabeth. But in this vast circle, with all of us holding hands, looking from one witch to the next, I see that we are transformed, wearing blankets and shawls and hooded robes instead of jackets. Looking around the circle from witch to witch, I also scan for my camp buddy, the witch who kindly e-mailed me in the months prior to camp, offering tips and guidelines to make my stay more meaningful, if not comfortable. During our correspondence she answered all of my questions, but there is one I have been saving to ask her in person: Of all the names in the world, why has she chosen to go by Lilith? Each of the witches has chosen something other than her given name by which to be known at camp. I'm still working on mine, but my camp buddy has chosen one with a loaded history.

But I can't find her. After asking around, it becomes apparent that the search will not be simple: Each witch I question points out a different Lilith, none of them my own. There are Liliths here and Liliths there, pretty much everywhere. We are awash in women who go by the oldest name in the book of evil.

In the beginning there was contradiction. Just try reading Genesis. In the first chapter, God created man and woman in his own image. Both from dust. He tells them to be fruitful, to go multiply. This was on the sixth day. Not much later in the same chapter, it is stated that it is not good that man should be alone and that, in fact, he needs a "help meet." For some unexplained reason, God then causes Adam to fall into a deep sleep, removes a rib from the first man, and makes woman, after which Adam refers to her, saying, "This is now bone of my bones, and flesh of my flesh: she shall be called Woman, because she was taken out of Man."

The "this is now" part of Adam's quote leads me to believe that the first woman, the one we know as Lilith, must have been a doozie. What happened to her, the one made from dust, the same stuff of Adam—his equal?

According to Raphael Patai, scholar and author of *The Hebrew Goddess*, the earliest written mention of Lilith is probably from about 2400 B.C.E., in the Sumerian King list, a text in the Sumerian language compiled by scribes and listing the rulers of Sumer. Lilith then appears in the Sumerian epic *Gilgamesh and the Huluppu Tree*, dating from around 2000 B.C.E., as well as in a Babylonian terracotta relief somewhat contemporary with the poem.

The Old Testament began to be recorded sometime around 1500 B.C.E. While the authorship of the first books may be forever debated, they are popularly attributed to Moses, who is believed to have lived sometime between 1500 and 1300 B.C.E., though the events related—the Creation and the flood, for instance—are believed to have happened long before his life on Earth. By the time the first symbols were scratched or pressed onto clay tablets, the great civilization of the Sumerians had been absorbed into a Semitic state, and left behind were their writing system (cuneiform) and many aspects of their religion. One of the latter was Lilith, who slithered her way into the oblique Genesis references through storytelling, in many tales becoming so directly associated with the epic serpent that she is interpreted as being him. In her snakelike persona, Lilith also has a strong association with a lamia, Greek mythology's fabulous female monster with the head and breasts of a woman and the body of a serpent. Both of these mythological females share other associations, as well—of being vampires with a thirst for the blood of children, and redheads.

A harlot as well as a vampire, Lilith never lets her lovers

go but never supplies any real satisfaction, either; eternally dangling the prospect of desire but forever withholding the money shot. And it was sex that broke up her marriage to Adam, or so it was said during the Talmudic period (the second through fifth centuries C.E.), when the Jewish faith taught that she was Adam's first wife. Apparently, the first couple found no joy together after Adam approached her for sex and she refused to lie beneath him. "Why should I lie beneath you," she is said to have asked, as quoted in Patai's book, "when I am your equal, since both of us were created from dust?"

Refusing to be overpowered, Lilith invoked the name of God and flew away to the Red Sea, a place known to harbor "lascivious demons." There, she began a promiscuous life-style that ensures her role as a force of real religious and moral reckoning well into the nineteenth century, shaping the conduct of countless people by providing a conscious image of the quintessential evil woman. In his book, Patai goes so far as to make the point that a citizen of Sumer in 2500 B.C.E. would have very little in common with a nineteenth-century East European Hasidic Jew except, per-haps, the ability to easily recognize the role of Lilith in their lives. And her role is strong. We hardly need another like her, so pervasive is her message.

Her myth is part terror, part reinforcement, like the Gilgamesh epic which was told and told again until finally it was written down, the details providing the key to remembering the moral lesson from each telling to the next, ensuring it through repetition. Of course we can identify her by the universal fears she speaks to in the human conscious-ness, but to ensnare that fear and laminate it into our souls, it would help to see her, somehow, in daily use. That device would enable something resembling a shock, a little reminder, a little prick of conscience in an everyday kind of way.

Perhaps this role of Lilith is best illustrated by what was found during an excavation by University of Pennsylvania researchers. Fifty miles southeast of Hilla, Iraq, dozens of bowls dating from about C.E. 600 were unearthed. These were the belongings of the common people—cereal bowls, salad bowls, everyday ware. Depicted on many are ideas that pervaded the thoughts of the sixth-century Jewish colony at Nippur. On these so-called Nippur bowls, Lilith can be seen etched naked, with long, untamed hair, perky breasts, and very visible genitals. In the accompanying texts on the bowls, which are exhortations intended to protect the owners, she is portrayed as a succubus, lurking in arches and doorways, at night joining men in their beds and producing demonic offspring from nocturnal emissions. Jealous—always jealous—she despises the children born of her victims and sucks their blood or strangles them and, swooping in on the most morbid fear of humans, she wrenches fetuses from the womb and leaves women barren.

Lilith is unique in the pantheon of human fright. Born before the first sin, she is not cursed with the sentence of death. In fact, she will never die. And, having escaped before that fateful act of Eve, Lilith is not subject to the rules we live by. There is nowhere she cannot go and there's nothing to be done about it. Except to be vigilant. We are meant to be able to identify her and live within the bookends of that fear, remembering at all times that women should not refuse to lie beneath men and that men should not pick someone who might.

Even with all the power of her history behind her,

however, in order to be remembered, Lilith needs to be recognized, rendered unforgettably. And she was—as a redhead.

As the longest-running she-demon in history, Lilith's identity spread like fire, leaping through cultures, her myth being reinforced for thousands of years from the Nippur bowls to countless later interpretations in the visual and performing arts, appearing as a woman's face on a red-haired serpent in myriad renderings of the temptation scene, including on the ceiling of the Sistine Chapel by Michelangelo, in *Original Sin* by Hugo van der Goes, as well as in *The Fall of Man* by Titian. Her face also appears as that of the serpent in cold stone, in a frieze on Paris's Notre Dame. But her most famous portrait is by pre-Raphaelite painter Dante Gabriel Rossetti, in which her purling hair is a subject in itself, portrayed in a vibrant shade of red.

The lineage of Lilith's very name is disputed, though all its roots are dark. Most rabbinic literature etymologically associates Lilith with *layelah*, the Hebrew word for night, though some scholars believe it is more likely that the name traveled to us in the Hebraized form of *Lilitu*, the same name used for a Babylonian storm spirit. In all, she is an icon in the history of the world of red hair, the oldest female cornerstone on which to build an argument for the evil and sexually charged identity of the red-haired woman.

Yet, when we view Lilith in contemporary feminist society, she has been transformed to a sort of goddess, or Goddess. The Lilith Institute on the West Coast is named for her; its mission is to promote the study of sacred text, myth, and ritual. A Jewish feminist quarterly begun in 1976 is called *Lilith, the Independent Women's Magazine*. She has traveled over time and continents and cultures, all the way to that standard-bearer of tastes, contemporary American television, where she lives on in reruns of one of the longest-running shows, *Cheers*, and its spin-off, *Frazier*, in that medium's history—and then as a self-absorbed, cold-as-ice female psychiatrist (lovely in its terror, a woman who sees into your id) named, of course, Lilith. In the television rendition, however, she is played for laughs and she is played by a brunette.

And then there are the witches who honor Lilith by taking her name. For the women in the circle whose hands I am holding, she is a symbol of women's unity, freedom of choice, and sexuality. She is the "She Who Will Not Lie Beneath" ideal to these women: Lilith is sexual freedom, personified. Indeed, there is a dominatrix in San Francisco who advertises on the Web for her slap-and-spank shop called Lady Lilith's Dungeon. Yes, she's a redhead.

Revisionism is part of the reason that some of history's nastier stories get a good scrubbing-up; we clean them to the point where they reflect our own faces in a preferable light. But there is something more than revision at work with the identity of redheaded women. That something comes into view when tracing backward from the idea of redheads as a group and how we feel about them to how they were identified in ancient references. And it is fueled by more than the venom added in the portrayal of enemies or by how we put out own qualities into our representations of our gods.

As we trace backward in time, what quickly becomes apparent is that there is no such thing as "all redheads." Redheads are not considered equal. Somewhere in time the identity of red hair split evenly along the lines of gender; after the divide, the red-haired woman evolved from being merely evil to being highly sexualized while the red-haired man's development got arrested soon after something in his presence poisoned the well for all red-haired men. Red-haired men simply do not make us feel the way we do when we are in the presence of red-haired women.

I knew this to be true from my own experience. My red-haired father's identity was very different from mine. He was considered good-looking *in spite* of having red hair; the root of my desirability has always seemed braided to my red hair. While my lovers had varying levels of appreciations of the trait, all had at least some. At witch camp, a part of me begins to feel the elemental propinquity of the personal part of this tale, of how my identity was cast under this red lens, as well. I begin to feel like I am tracking myself.

I had never given much thought to the meaning of my own red hair. Thinking about it on either the macro or micro level—about redheads in general or redheaded relatives and if any of their associated traits trickled down to me—I couldn't see much past the done deal: I was born a redhead and remain so. But giving myself the assignment to consider the identity of the red head, a personal fulcrum—a moment in time when the meaning of my color changed from one hue to another—helped me see the historical moment when things tipped for all of us with red hair. And after the tip, came the great divide between men and women of my color.

When I was a child there was frequent teasing about my red hair; as I got older it morphed into an object of desire. The evolution in the attitudes of others began when I was maturing into a woman. The moment of intuition was when I watched Stephen, my first serious boyfriend, write a summertime letter to his school roommate. In the note, meeting me was related in the innocent gushing phrases of adolescence that ended with "and she is a *redhead*." As he wrote it, I instantly realized that my status had been upped; that I had been transposed into someone to desire and that one of my means of passage was the very color of my hair. After passing into the enigmatic arena of sexual desire—both mine and his—there was no going back.

It would be unreasonable to say that my earlier playground teasings had been intolerable or cruel. Growing up in the New York City school system, I had witnessed unfair tauntings over other human pigmentary traits. Mine never approached the torment imbedded in those. While they were annoying—"Carrot top!" "Redhead!"—they were hardly reasons to get into a rock fight. And later, the "red-in-the-head, hot-in-the-bed" saying was always laid out more as an invitation than an accusation.

Unlike black skin, red hair does not identify those of us who have it as being part of a people whose history is told with the predominant theme of wretched discrimination. And although there were red-haired slaves kept by the Romans, and a woeful history of hatred of the Irish, with whom red hair is strongly associated, redheads are so rare that it is most likely their scarcity, more than any other quality, that makes them targets of contemporary teasing. It may very well be this same dearth that originally left them open to fear and loathing.

Or was it fear *or* loathing? When ancient reactions to red hair divided along gender lines, they also split into separate reactions: the fear traveling with red-haired women and the loathing with red-haired men. But like the legend of Lilith herself, along the time line of history, redheaded women were not only feared but became associated with desire as well, both being states of heightened arousal. In this, red-haired women loosely resemble a thermometer, their collective red line descending as the surrounding environment cools. Conversely, when responding to redheaded men, humans fevered right along the emotional spectrum at abhorrence. That's not true in every case, of course, or redheads would have died out as quickly as they appeared. But clearly the relative heat affected the male-female divide in our responses.

Looking to explore this idea of a sexual divide, I sought the single greatest concentration of famous redheads and found them among British monarchs.

The first recorded red-haired British monarch was a woman. She was a Celtic warrior, a queen. Her name was Boudicca and she led her people, the Iceni, against the Romans in the C.E. 60s. She was married to Prasutagus, king of the Iceni in the C.E. 40s. Far fewer facts are known of her husband than of the passionate, powerful queen. What is known is that Roman general Julius Caesar invaded Celtic Britain in 55 to 54 B.C.E. but failed to conquer it and that in C.E. 43, under Emperor Claudius, the Romans succeeded. After Boudicca and Prasutagus married, they had two daughters, though history does not record their names. By C.E. 50, Prasutagus was a leader in a rebellion of tribes in southeastern Britain against the Romans. Despite being quickly crushed, the king was allowed to keep his lands but was reduced to the status of client-king. Then he died, leaving Boudicca, not yet thirty, and her young daughters half of his vast property, the other half going to the Romans.

Everything changed under the rule of Roman emperor Nero (C.E. 54 to 68), when local administrators seized the lands left to the women. But Boudicca fought back. As punishment, she was taken to a public space where she was stripped naked and beaten. Her daughters were raped.

The Iceni and many other Celtic tribes rallied around Boudicca, who called for a furious revenge and invoked the names of the gods to assist her. At the time Londinium was a city of about thirty thousand, consisting mostly of merchants and their families. Built on banks of the River Thames, it was a thriving city to which trading ships brought ideas and goods from all over the Roman Empire. It would later be called London, but not before Boudicca slaughtered its Roman residents and burned the city to the ground.

Riding her chariot, leading her army of what some estimates say was a hundred thousand, she is described by Dio Cassius as follows: "Huge of frame, terrifying of aspect, and with a harsh voice. A great mass of bright red hair fell to her knees: she wore a great twisted golden necklace, and a tunic of many colours, over which was a thick mantle, fastened by a brooch. Now she grasped a spear, to strike fear into all who watched her." And in that description she is strongly associated with a banshee, a Celtic mythical creature, frequently depicted with long red hair, whose wailing always foretells an imminent human death. In some modern accounts, *banshee* is the word used to describe the female members of Queen Boudicca's army as they ran screaming into battle.

Eventually Boudicca lost the fight. Rather than face another public humiliation and, this time, certain death, she managed to escape with her children. It is believed that in a private refuge she administered poison to her two daughters and then drank it herself and died.

These days gorgeous images of Boudicca can be viewed throughout Great Britain, the most famous in London. She is portrayed as a heroic symbol of Britain, now in bronze, on the Thames Embankment, appearing to advance on the Houses of Parliament. The rumor is that her body is buried somewhere along the embankment of the great river, which makes her seem even more powerful; her restless bones, shifting in the changing silt of the banks. The massive statue is a striking image of her and her two daughters astride an enormous chariot, charging into battle. It's a glorious piece of art and one that receives a regular ritual dousing and anointment, resulting in the occasional arrest of local pagans.

Nor is she forgotten elsewhere in contemporary culture. In the 2005 fashion collections a once-struggling English design firm is catwalking its way into the mainstream under the name Boudicca. Its public relations material revamps the tale of the powerful queen into one of a contemporary, sexy style maven. Similarly, the story of the queen is retold in children's books and historical texts in more enamored tones than would seem possible to portray a warrior-queen who brutally annihilated her enemies.

Boudicca was hardly the last redheaded British monarch. There was William II (1087–1100), who earned the names Rufus and William Red either because of his red hair or his angry disposition. He was followed by the Angevins (as in Anjou), a good-looking bunch of strong redheads who provided England with a dynasty of remarkable kings, the Plantagenets, for 331 years. In fact, that particular line was begat by the mating of two redheads, the hot-tempered Henry II (1154–1189), who married Eleanor of Aquitaine (think *The Lion in Winter*, starring Katharine Hepburn and

Peter O'Toole). Their descendants began a line leading from the strawberry blond Richard the Lionheart through kings of England and queens of Sicily and Castile, a Holy Roman Emperor, kings of Castile and Jerusalem, and a king of France, thereby spreading that redheaded Angevin gene over great land masses of civilization.

Later, during the reign of the House of Tudor (from Henry VII to Elizabeth I), red hair appeared on three monarchs in a row, all of whom also are associated with having blood either ringing their necks or on their hands. Of the three, Lady Jane Grey was the first. The nine-days' Queen, she was the granddaughter of Mary Tudor, the red-haired sister of the red-haired Henry VIII. Henry, as we know, had six wives. ("Divorced, beheaded, died. Divorced, beheaded, survived" is the rhyme taught to English school-children to remember the queens' fates.) Lady Jane was ordered beheaded by red-haired, Catholic Mary I, the elder daughter of Henry VIII, who died childless, opening the way for the Protestant Virgin Queen Elizabeth I, who wore her long red hair unadorned and down to denote her virginity at her coronation. The second daughter of Henry VIII and Anne Boleyn (beheaded), she was the first woman to rule alone since the twelfth century's Queen Matilda. Elizabeth's forty-five-year reign, the Elizabethan era, is considered one of the most glorious periods in the history of England, despite her ordered execution of her cousin, Mary Queen of Scots, a lock of whose red hair is on display at Holyrood Palace in Edinburgh.

An artifact on its own, in a locket, behind a museum case, however, suggests so much but tells us so little. And it was here that my theory of the sexual divide of redheads might have petered out. Even viewed in light of the fact that the

English were ruled by so many bloody and bloodied red-heads, it was impossible to conclude anything more than that red hair was a Tudor trademark. Looking at the red-haired bloodlines and matching them to time lines, or viewing a locket of hair, has all the depth of skimming stones unless you take into account what buoys that tale—what people believed in at the time the lock was cut, what they feared, what gods they invoked to help them, or how they spoke.

After the end of Elizabeth's long reign in the early 1600s, another flash of red appears in the use of the word *pixie*, which emerged in southwest England. These ingenious little sprites, also known as piskies, are strongly associated with fairies, a widely defined group of spirits that can be either good or evil. The belief in fairies in sixteenth-century England should not be underestimated; their widespread acceptance can be compared to the Greeks' belief in what we consider to be their mythical gods. Pixies have always been predominantly redheaded (though in *Harry Potter and the Chamber of Secrets*, the second Harry Potter movie, the Cornish pixies are portrayed in blue) and can be found in fields. In popular usage the pixie and fairy have become somewhat interchangeable, but not before creating an impression that red hair carries with it otherworldly talents.

A tradition of a belief in such talents makes sense in its Elizabethan time, as it is a hallmark of what is known as sympathetic magic, a belief that things can act on each other at a distance and that disparate elements such as stars, patterns in entrails, leaves of tea, and the lines of one's palm are magically connected to one's life. In turn, sympathetic magic somewhat explains the Chapman quote about the fat of a redhead as an essential ingredient for poison: If a red-haired man was venomous, he could infect someone who partook of him, exemplifying the organic acceptance of the connection between the outer world and humankind.

The red-haired man is deadly as poison, plain and frightening. And it is William Shakespeare who tells us why. Shakespeare was the voice of his time, a living product of a Catholic family whose beliefs were unseated during his lifetime by a revolution of Protestantism. Both those religions struggled mightily against the ingrained symbols and prophecies of sympathetic magic. So pervasive were these prophecies in his time that the date of Queen Elizabeth's coronation was plotted by an astrologer.

In act III, scene 4 of Shakespeare's *As You Like It*, Rosalind says Orlando's hair is "of the dissembling colour," in an effort to shake off her love for him. Celia, her cousin and companion, adjusts the image, suggesting that the hair is "something browner than Judas's," which, after more banter, makes everything all right again. This bit of dialogue hurtles us back thousands of years in its meaning, back to Judas, as well as exactly captures its significance at the time it was written. And in literature, it is followed by a slightly later reference written by poet and playwright John Dryden (1631–1700), about his bookseller—which, at the time, was the same as being one's publisher. Dryden had asked for an advance of money, which Jacob Tonson, the bookseller, refused, for the poet was already in arrears. Dryden did what writers do: He wrote about his disappointment, describing Tonson as being "with leering looks, bull-faced and freckled hair / With two left legs / with Judas-coloured hair, and Frowzy pores that taint the ambient air."

By the time of these writings, red-haired men and red-headed women had parted company. The split can be seen in what they carried in their kiss. While Lilith was evil through her powers of seduction, it was those powers that also gave her a highly sexualized identity, even at the height of her ancient ability to provoke fear. Lilith's kiss brought seduction, with all of its possibilities. No promise to lie beneath, perhaps, but still, the lure of sex. On the lips of Judas, on the other hand, lay the kiss from the original poisoner of the well, that kiss of betrayal, the kiss of death.

But exactly how far back to plot the themes that colorize Judas's kiss, as well as Shakespeare's and Dryden's inflammatory views, remained unclear to me until one night at witch camp, when the original fiery redheaded male—the first and most profound of them all—was hurled directly into our path.

The theme of the weeklong witch camp is Isis and Osiris, and a selection of the deities aligned with them, some of whom are more obvious in their lineage than others. Isis, the Egyptian goddess of fertility, is the wife of Osiris, the Egyptian king of the dead.

Every night after dinner the witches at camp process up the hill for what is known as Ritual. Beginning after sundown, and going late into the night, the teachers among us take turns invoking various gods and goddesses, peeling incantations aloft into the wind that funnels down the craggy Vermont valley as the witches ring and spiral around a massive bonfire. It is as dark a night as I have ever witnessed, the nearest town nowhere to be seen and no lights visible anywhere in the vast camp. Leaving the blaze of the fire means plotting a dead reckoning through the pitch-black woods back to our sleeping bags. The night is cold. A witch steps out and screams the name of Set.

The crowd roars.

Set, god of chaos, confusion, storms, winds, the desert, and foreign lands. Set, who is represented throughout the history of mythology as a redhead.

"Set!" the crowd is chanting, "Set, Set, Set!" And the assembly surges forward.

In a whirl of people and robes, the crashing of the fire snaps huge sparks into the night sky. The shouting and wind-drenched crowd is impelled against the heat. Set, redheaded god. The hooded and caped crowd is goading Set to show himself, to step forward through the dead of night. O Set. The witch invokes his name again, and again the crowd repeats it, screaming. The fire pitches up toward the black sky and two hundred people rear back, shrieking.

"Set!" the witch cries again as I grab Mary Elizabeth's forearm, knowing that the witches are calling for the red-headed devil himself.

CHAPTER TWO

The Old Poker and the Inhabitants of Pandemonium

*It Is in His Kiss—and in Our Blood—
to Fear the Red-Haired Man*

"EVERYONE STANDS IN HORROR," Jean-Baptist
Thiers, a seventeenth-century French scholar, said
about red hair, "because Judas, it is said, was red-haired."
And so he appears through centuries, in art and in representations onstage.

Biblical scholars suggest that the surname Iscariot refers
to Judas being a man of Kerioth, a northern Judea town,
and that he is "the son of Simon." His motive for betraying
Christ cannot be definitely stated, though thirty pieces of
silver change hands at varying times in various versions.
What also is not stated in the Bible is the hair color of Judas;
nowhere in its pages is he said to be red-haired.

A proverb tells us that the devil is in the details, and in the
case of red hair and Judas, it's true; for this reference, we
must look to the devil himself. As portrayed in the Gospels
of Luke and John, an evil spirit instigates the traitorous

bargain that results in the betrayal of Christ. John is more specific, saying that it is the devil who enters the heart of Judas. But lacking any real biblical reference to his hair color, making the red-hair connection to Judas in the pages of John requires that we believe in sympathetic magic— more specifically, that when a person is entered by the devil, some part of the victim turns red.

Hair color aside, the death of Judas is associated with the color red, despite the fact that in some versions his end was reportedly a bloodless hanging from a tree while in other versions his guts were dashed from his body. To this day, the *Cercis siliquastrum*, an ornamental shrub or tree native to southern Europe and western Asia, holds the popular name the Judas Tree. Legend holds that it is the kind of tree from which Judas hanged himself; the redbud, its North American relative, also bears the betrayer's name. When in bloom, both are resplendent with reddish-purple flowers, the latter, in my gardening zone and in both my front and back yards, coming into flower after Easter.

The Gospel according to John was written after the life of Jesus, possibly in the last decade of the first century C.E. If it was composed with the unspoken understanding that when the devil enters a person, some part of the victim turns red, then several supporting beliefs would also need to be in place. Along with the conviction that being entered by the devil transforms a person in such a colorful manner, there also would need to be a belief in a strong link between one's color and one's character, and that the first identifies qualities of the second.

By the time the Bible was being written, there existed strong beliefs about red hair as well as implications about the character of its bearer. This is documented in the appearance of red-wigged actors playing slaves in Roman comedies. The influence of the Romans is vast, their dominance not declining until into the fourth century C.E., their empire eventually reaching from Great Britain through Egypt, from Spain to the Euphrates. For the purposes of the history of red hair and the Romans' mark on it, those wigs not only signal the presence of beliefs about red hair but also make a connection to the historic discrimination against the Jews.

At its simplistic worst, the fear and hatred of the Jews, so tragically visible throughout history, boils down to the accusation that they killed Christ. The story of the most infamous murder in history includes Judas, the man who betrayed Christ and who, in history's view, was a redhead. Our contemporary feelings about red-haired men connect to the identity of Judas through those wigs. To understand that connection requires first linking the few existing historic markers about men and red hair to one another. These include the Chapman quote about poison, the Shakespeare quote about a dissembling color, Judas himself, and the Romans' red-haired theatrical wigs. After making this link, the entire line of thinking must be associated to the origins of the idea that color bespeaks character.

The first connection, linking only those historic markers, can be made on the head of Shylock, Shakespeare's moneylender in *The Merchant of Venice*. That the play was written as a comedy is frequently forgotten. These days, the vicious anti-Semitic sentiment rendered in the drama gives the audience little breathing space in which to find the humor. But in its time it was intended to inform, if not please, an anti-Semitic audience, which Shakespeare's contemporary viewers most assuredly were.

At the debut of *The Merchant of Venice*, England had been officially without Jews for three hundred years, following their expulsion in 1290. During Shakespeare's tenure the Jews continued to be forbidden to return on threat of death, and it was not until 1656 that they were readmitted. So few, if any, in the English audience viewing Shylock at his 1590s debut had ever seen any Jewish person other than this staged character. In order to portray a Jewish man onstage and make his presence known and understood, what was required was an easily identifiable costume, one that had been established before Shakespeare ever set pen to paper. The bard couldn't make it up. If he had, no one would have recognized the symbolism, understood the intended identity of the character, and applied the stereotypes needed to follow the plot. So, Shakespeare laid his hands on what had gone before him.

The character of Shylock appears in one of three famous sixteenth-century plays in which similar devices are supplied by the playwright to guide the audience to recognize and understand the character of the Jewish role. In all three, the very identity of the role being played depends on these devices. In *The Merchant of Venice*, Robert Wilson's *Three Ladies of London*, and Christopher Marlowe's *The Jew of Malta*, a man in the form of a usurer, or money lender, appears, each time as a Jew, and in each of the original productions, as well as those for some time after, he does so wearing a red wig.

The usury theme in Shakespeare follows those plays by Wilson and Marlowe. In *The Merchant of Venice*, a young Christian man borrows money from a Jewish usurer but is unable to repay it in the designated three months' time. When Antonio, the borrower, cannot repay the loan, Shylock, the lender, insists on the pound of flesh agreed upon in the original bargain. Portraying Shylock in the money-lending line of work is more contemporary to Shakespeare's time than is the visual cue of the wig. Usury was the main occupation open to the Jews at the time of their expulsion, and it was the crown outlawing the practice that directly led to the Jews being turned out of England.

The representation of Shylock in the red wig has direct roots in the morality plays, which, along with the mystery play and the miracle play, were the popular forms of drama in the Middle Ages. More than anything, the morality plays were a transitional step from religious drama to secular plays and thus are colored by aspects of both. Short and serious in tone, the morality plays employed allegory and taught moral lessons. Through the use of actors personifying human qualities—Gluttony, Charity, Vice, for instance—the plays argued for a moral life. And it is in these morality plays of the Middle Ages that Jews frequently appeared as diabolical, under a hair color which, by then, had long associations with the characteristic trait of treachery.

The theatrical tradition of red wigs is therefore very much a statement of the character of the people who wear them. In the Middle Ages, the diabolical traits represented by the wigs were those of a person who took the position of opposing, or was presented as an alternative to, Christ—or, as it is stated in popular usage, the Antichrist. However, belief in Judas as the Antichrist does not have universal acceptance. What you believe about Jesus and whether or not he is Christ will drive your thoughts about alternatives to his teachings. Christians may believe that the Antichrist has yet to come—his appearance must precede that of the day of the Lord, according to Thessalonians—or that the Antichrist has already visited and done his dirty work. The latter idea is written in John, who sees the "one destined for destruction" not as someone in our future but as Judas Iscariot. But, no matter. Those who await the coming of the Antichrist as well as those who believe we live in the wake of his evil work have in common a vivid color in which to portray those who oppose God: red.

Red became a color of the soldiers of the Antichrist and consequently red became the color to represent the Jews in morality plays. Another physical characteristic seen on Judas and worn by the usurer in the sixteenth-century English plays is a huge, grotesque nose, which also enters the stage via the diabolical, although the length of the nose has varying attributions, including the pulling of Satan's nose by the red-hot tongs of St. Dunstan, a tenth-century archbishop of Canterbury.

According to Ruth Mellinkoff, a noted art historian, the first inklings of what is now known to art historians as a recognizable Judas—long-nosed and red-haired—can be seen in the visual arts beginning as early as the ninth century C.E., when his image began to be colored, filled in, and shaped by various artists in far-flung places. The intent of the portraitists was to identify Judas to the viewer, using over time such diverse identifiers as the hooked nose, a ruddy complexion, and red hair, the presence of a money purse, and the wearing of a yellow robe. These defining characteristics traveled, like gossip, and eventually over-lapped. By the sixteenth century, familiar examples of this version of Judas are seen in the visual arts throughout Europe. The highest concentration of incidents of Judas with red hair appear in German art from the fourteenth through sixteenth centuries. These include two arresting portraits of a bright red-haired Judas by Bertram of Minden, *Last Supper* and *Betrayal of Christ*, from the early 1300s. Later, Gaspard Isenmann makes Judas truly grotesque in a painting titled *Betrayal and Arrest of Christ*, in which the artist depicts the giver of the infamous kiss with a huge hooked nose, ropey red hair, and an unseemly open mouth.

In her work Dr. Mellinkoff also cites the best example of the identity's spread and subsequent transition to a fixed image of Judas as a circa 1515 *Last Supper*, the work of an unknown Burgundian painter. Here the artist applies all the options on his palette—the purse, the yellow robe, the red hair, and the hooked nose—gathering together on one canvas all these physical traits and rendering them into the image of a single, hated man whose character is widely understood.

It was the expectation of the Antichrist that pervaded the beliefs of the Middle Ages and the sixteenth and seventeenth centuries. This idea of heightened anticipation coincided with—as well as colorized—the morality plays, which, in their time, gave way to the works of William Shakespeare and his peers. The negative stereotyping used by the Romans when identifying slaves under red wigs in comic productions lived on in this tradition, and for Shakespeare's audience, Shylock's red wig signaled a dual message of the presence of evil and the presence of someone who is absurd, as is a jester or a fool. We are to be amused at *The Merchant of Venice*, for it is a comedy. But as with the derisive humor the Romans directed at the slaves, Shakespeare's lines were intended to make audiences laugh *at* Shylock, not *with* him. Together these fearful-foolish portrayals of the Jew became an effective way in which to both shade and nuance the anti-Semitism that shadows Christianity throughout its history. The red wig is in no way alone in its role but rather part of a long and evil history of some people requiring other people to identify their religious beliefs in their dress.

A vivid picture of what evil looks like when the opposing forces of good and evil go to war can be seen in the book of Revelation. Viewed by some believers to be a message from Jesus through his angel to John, the final book of the Bible begins in letter form and comes to an astonishing climax in chapter 19's battle between the Lamb of God and Satan's emissary, the Antichrist, as well as those who bear the mark of Satan. And although the primitive origins of the very name of Satan are hotly debated—in the Hebrew Bible, the word is used to refer to anyone who plays the role of enemy or accuser—what is known is that by the third century B.C.E., the idea of an archenemy of God appears. The New Testament supplies several names for this character and is probably the source for the popularization, if not the standardization, of the name Satan, as well as for the idea that Satan and his henchmen, known as demons, may enter into others to inflame evil deeds and those demons carry his mark.

The idea of evil is as old as mankind's ability to fear the unknown, the dark, illness, and death. From those fears arise beliefs, providing every human culture in their history on Earth with faith in the thing beyond their ability to understand, in how to identify that thing, and in methods with which to negotiate with those forces. Over time and through communication, some ideas gain greater influence. As a result of either neighborly proximity or because of war, and the triumph of one people over another, cultures assimilate into one another. And even cultures in struggle borrow ideas. In the case of magic, supernaturalism, and what we now call religion, the individualized polytheism of distinct cultures funneled into fewer and fewer existing religions, yielding fairly standardized versions of fear. And from those fearful ideas emerged our icons, which then gained acceptance. Among those ideas are how we identify as well as react to people with red hair.

By the time the Old Testament was written, red-haired people were on the earth in sufficient numbers to warrant significant mention. But with what associations? To find what had been written in the Bible about the hair color prior to the appearance of the New Testament Judas, we look to Esau and, later, King David, both viewed throughout history as redheads. Along with their hair color, they share the fact that they both made memorable marriages: Esau wed outside his culture when, in succession, he chose two Hittites, thereby greatly displeasing his parents; King David wed Bathsheba, also a Hittite, after he killed her husband Uriah, one of his own "mighty men," to cover up the adulterous affair with her. However, read separately and separated by so many pages, there seems small, if any, association between the Bible's version of these two men and Judas or the devil, other than their shared hair color. If we were to read only about Judas, would we ascribe to him the hair color of Esau and David, coloring in the lines to red? We would if we thought that when the devil entered him, some part of him turned red or if, believing that color connotes character, we saw him as the successor in a line of certain character flaws portrayed on the classic red-haired man.

Judas does not appear in the Bible until the New Testament Gospels. David appears in Samuel and Kings in the Old Testament. Esau precedes them both, appearing at the beginning, in Genesis. But early as he is, even Esau is not the original model of the biblical red-haired man.

When we first learn of Esau in the Bible, as he is struggling with his twin in their mother's womb, we are witnessing a wrestling match that will continue nearly all their lives. It is an eternal theme: sibling rivalry and its attendant horrors. And one that is well covered in the Bible, the first version appearing only verses prior to those portraying Esau. It is the story of Cain and Abel.

The firstborn of Adam and Eve, Cain and his brother Abel are perhaps twins. Cain becomes a farmer; Abel, a shepherd. When Cain offers a sacrifice of his crop to Yahweh, it is rejected. Cain then murders Abel and is found out by Yahweh, who condemns Cain despite his protestations of innocence. As his punishment, Cain is sentenced to wander the earth, which he does in a land called Nod, east of Eden. Before he goes, Cain pleads for mercy, which is granted by Yahweh, who places a sign on Cain that both protects him from being murdered and marks him for who he is. The sign given to Cain by Yahweh is unspecified in the Bible, though in popular culture it is believed to be red hair.

That in the beginning there was red hair and that it was both a blessing and a curse is a hellish way to start the story of mankind. And protected though he was, the negative aspect of his mark is what many people think of when they think of Cain. His name can be found amid only two other proper names listed in the thesaurus under the voluminous synonyms for *killing*. His story continues to be used as a warning of what one reaps through unchecked passion. In some interpretations of the story, Cain is identified as the son of either Satan or the wicked angel Sammael. In others, he is associated with that famous serpent in Eden.

Of Cain, Esau, David, and Judas, it is the last, the betrayer of Christ, who provides the reader of the Bible the most extreme case of the evil of falling prey to passionate wants. The story is told with such graphic clarity that perhaps the only question left open for individual interpretation is whether those wants were Judas's own or they were ignited when the devil entered him. If they were his own desires, they could be seen as those of a redhead. Choosing the bedeviled version, the colorization is the same. But can we be trusted to remember the evil of Judas if we don't leave the hair color/mark of the devil on him? Perhaps not, and so we tell it that way, sing it that way, cuneiform it, draw it and paint it, needlepoint, fresco, stain glass, and watercolor it that way. Somehow, Judas's hair was turned to red and when it was, he was singled out in the picture, easily identified by it and forever after, with it.

After reading in the Bible, some of us might close the Good Book with only mild associations about red hair, with little more than the knowledge that some Jewish characters in it had red hair. Other readers might think that those red-haired Jews were innately passionate and that their passions got them in trouble. Those readers inclined to look for clues to the identity of the redhead could find them in the Bible's pages and tell their friends. The conclusions you make all depend on what you want from the story of red hair, who you are going to tell it to, and why.

What I wanted was something older than Judas, and it had led me to a pagan worship ceremony on a cold dark night, atop a windswept hill in Vermont. Along with the frigid temperature, real fear is all I can register when the original evil red-haired man is hurled in my path.

The bonfire crowd surges toward the heat while invoking the name of Set. I lunge backward, grabbing Mary Elizabeth's forearm, refusing to be part of a circle of people calling for the devil himself. Not a bit torn between reporting and participating, I am ready to bolt. There, on a bald hill, closing in on midnight, with two hundred witches, one reporter and her friend, most chanting, screaming, and dancing around a massive bonfire, all I can picture are the gentle good folk of Vermont grabbing their ax handles and pitchforks and making for our hardscrabble hill to alter the evil of our ways. And that looks pretty good to me. Maybe we could hitch a ride out, I think. More terrifying is when I remember how very deep into the woods we had driven to get here; how there is not a twinkling of light from the nearest town, not a cell phone that works, not a line to the outside but one, in the kitchen, far down that dark path, somewhere off in the pitch black woods. Now, all I can feel is fear.

Mary Elizabeth has a great penchant toward reason, and slowly we move back toward the fire as it rears up in the wind, soaring into the sky, emboldening the crowd in its fervid incantations.

"Set!" they shriek. "Set! Set! Set!"

At the center of a rich and often confusing cycle of inextricably braided Egyptian myths is Osiris, the god of the dead, and Set, his jealous brother. In its simplest form, the story includes Isis, wife of Osiris, and Horus, their son. While it is unknown when the beliefs in each myth began, it is known that from the beginning Egyptians were loyal to what is now referred to as the "god of the city," literally worshipping locally until the gods from more influential cities caught on. What is also known is that when Menes, the king, united the two lands that were Egypt, Horus, the god of the north, triumphed over Set and became the national god of Upper Egypt. This was about 3000 B.C.E.

In varying versions of the tale, it is claimed that Set tore himself from his mother's womb, burst through her side to be born; that when he grew up he murdered and dismembered Osiris, his own brother, on Midsummer's Day, and became the evil uncle to Horus. In some stories Set cuts his brother's body into either fourteen or sixteen pieces and floats it down the Nile. What remains consistent from one version to the next is the color of Set's hair. It is red.

On Earth, Osiris had many followers, the more vengeful of whom are said to have used redheads as sacrificial victims and buried them alive in homage to their god. Other interpretations of these sacrifices suggest that in an act of sympathetic magic, red-haired men were burned and their ashes scattered with winnowing fans in offerings by kings at the grave of Osiris. Sometimes victims are stand-ins for Osiris in his role as god of corn, which itself dies and comes to life each year, the ashes intended to promote the growth of the crops, the redheaded victims presenting the most viable impersonation of the ruddy grain.

Either way, it was hell to be a redhead in ancient Egypt. During the high point of Set's popularity, redheads were considered foreigners. Over time this idea of redheads being strangers got Set relegated to watching over borders, specifically those of the desert, as the personification of aridity and as the god of anyone alien. This arid association, though, also speaks of infertility. Set had no children, Horus having torn off his testicles. Set tore out Horus's eye and sexually abused him. Set was bisexual in some versions, and had to give back Horus's eye in others. Some tales have him seizing the souls of the unwary in the underworld. It is generally believed that red animals as well as redheaded people were his followers, red being a color of evil to the Egyptians.

Ramses II (of the nineteenth dynasty, 1200s B.C.E.) and his father, Seti I, both had red hair and brought around a resurgence of Set, aligning themselves with the god of chaos and worshipping his violent nature to further their own warring ways. Ramses named a division of his army for Set. It is known that Set's followers wore red, the dye for which came from the common plant Rubiaceae, a family of chiefly tropical and subtropical herbs, shrubs, and trees. One of the most common among them is madder (*Rubia tinctorum*), the roots of which have the highest concentration of the color and were used thousands of years ago—as evidenced by the pieces of red cloth found in Egyptian tombs, most particularly in those who had been followers of Set. Contemporary examination has revealed that madder was the dye used to color these cloths red.

Set and his revered evil have global associations that fling him far and wide. Set is identified with the Greek Typhon, the terrifying father of hot, dangerous winds (thus, the word *typhoon*) who was known to have a grisly rage, exhibited by the molten red rocks spewing from his many gaping mouths. Redheaded men sacrificed in the name of Typhon are believed to have been killed in an act of vengeance against him and in support of his enemy, Osiris. Evidence exists that red oxen were sacrificed by the Egyptians in spring, as were red-haired puppies killed by the Romans, as stand-ins for the corn spirit to make the grain turn red or golden. Belief in Set even extends to the Vikings. In one version of Set's tale, the redheaded demon goes on to live with Re, or Ra, the sun god, and becomes the voice of thunder. In this he is associated with the Germanic god Thor, the god of thunder, who is also depicted as a redhead and from whose red beard lightning was believed to originate. Thor's sacred creatures also include the red animals, such as the robin, fox, and squirrel. His following extended through the rise of the Vikings, well into the eleventh century, spreading as they did by ship more than five thousand miles on the globe in their three-hundred-year prominence.

Thor is with us still, every Thursday, the day named for him. While Thor contributed to the allure of the red-haired man—he had his good qualities, as well—Set contributed to the model for Christianity's idea of the devil: red-haired with red eyes, his animal form including long, pointed ears and a long snout. Among satanically inclined contemporary worshippers, Set is sometimes referred to as the "original devil."

The close of the tale of the greatness of ancient Egypt is the death of Cleopatra, whose henna-red hair suggests that the perception of red hair in her homeland had altered. The last ruler of the dynasty founded by Ptolemy, Cleopatra lived from 69 to 30 B.C.E., dying on her golden bed as Octavian's men broke down her boudoir door. With her death, the rule of Egypt fell to the Roman Empire, whose power did not wane until into the fourth century C.E. The Roman Empire absorbed many cultures, including those of Boudicca and Cleopatra, the two women representing the north-south points of the empire at its height. The Romans also absorbed Greek culture, whose great art, literature, and philosophy subsequently migrated throughout the empire—

as did those beliefs from all the people the Romans conquered. These beliefs included what people worshipped, what they feared, and what methods they employed to mitigate those fears, the strongest among those methods being humor.

The evil associations that were ascribed to red-haired men were in place at the height of ancient Egypt and appear to have traveled within the Roman Empire into morality plays and onto the Elizabethan stage. Along the way, historic anti-Semitism fed the flames of hatred to the extent needed to keep such vivid imagery alive. At the time of Shylock's debut, society's fears of the Jews illuminated the meaning of the wig. Then those fears waned somewhat, only to reappear repeatedly in history. In contemporary Western culture, such wigs can be seen on the heads of circus clowns.

But as the sentiments yielding distrust of the Jews as well as the power and meaning of red hair have waxed and waned, they also appear to have parted company. One is not currently dependent on the other, it would seem, yet the discrimination against redheads carries in its backstory the fear and hatred of the Jews as an unspoken alliance, an implicit undertone that easily goes unnoticed. More recent historic intolerance of redheads appears to arise less from the association with Jews than the notion that red hair is being worn by "others," outsiders, not of our own.

What does carry through time is the need for vigilance in identifying others. In their time, the wigs overrode any doubt about our inability to miss the Jewish character onstage. In this role they mirror the offstage version of the varying identifiers dating from the Middle Ages into the mid-twentieth century, requiring Jews to identify themselves by badges, hats, and yellow stars. These symbols attempt to counteract any effort of the part of the Jews to dissemble, to conceal their true role, by otherwise fitting in.

This prescription to identify oneself as being Jewish, and thereby be easily identified by others, was applied equally to both sexes. As Shakespeare used "dissembling" in *As You Like It*, it applied to men and women alike in their equal ability—or, possibly, intent—to provide a false or misleading appearance. Similarly, Judas is a form of scapegoat—a person made to bear the blame for others or to suffer in their place—and either sex can be one of those, as Judas stands in for all of his religion to anyone needing to believe that the Jews killed Christ. In the role of scapegoat Judas is strongly associated with demons, despite any argument over how he came by his treachery. The position of scapegoat is ancient, codified in a Day of Atonement ritual mentioned in Leviticus in which two goats are chosen by lot, one to be sacrificed for the Lord and the other sent to wander in the wilderness, carrying away the people's sins. The second goat was said to be sent for Azazel, who many modern scholars believe was a demon and whom Hebrew myth portrays as one of the demons seduced by Lilith.

Lilith and Judas. The difference in the meaning of their two kisses also exemplifies the similarity of the roles of the kissers: Both are but stand-ins for the devil, made to do his work. When Lilith fled the specter of a life spent lying under Adam, she flew to the Red Sea, a place known to harbor lascivious demons. She wanted to be among her own, with other demons, those deliverers of the devil's evil. We already know what happened to Judas, except perhaps to say that more than ever he appears like Lilith, in a supporting role. Both Lilith and Judas serve the devil, the evil one who spawned both male and female demons to perform his dirty work, and in doing so, colorized demons of both sexes, in red.

The devil and Judas had good, long runs onstage. Simultaneously tucked up under those red wigs, neither was seen nor heard though their ancient message was perceived by the audience. And, as with all major theatrical roles, they had an understudy, someone eagerly waiting in the wings to change places under the lights.

CHAPTER THREE

The Blood That
Scares the Hell into Us

Superstition, Taboo, and
the Blood That Divides Us

T HE SUCCESS OF the London theaters depended on each of them filling 1,500 to 2,000 seats each day. To do so required giving the people what they wanted to see. By the beginning of the seventeenth century, it appears that on the English stage the use of the scapegoat Jew, replete with red wig, had lost its power—possibly from overuse, possibly with the impending return of a Jewish population to London. Whatever the reason, the vividness of the stereotype got washed out. Waiting offstage, however, was a demon, ready for the role: the witch, who everyone agreed was evil, so stated in the English laws against witchcraft promulgated by Elizabeth I in 1563.

The role of witch quickly replaced the Jewish moneylender on the stage, such as in Shakespeare's *Macbeth*, written in 1606. And when it did, it represented two ways of thinking, one very old and the other contemporary with

Shakespeare. When the witch stepped in, the role of the red-haired woman was both transfused with the fear of an ancient taboo and mantled with a scapegoat's blame. The first, far older representation is more powerful and impossible to spot with the naked eye. By contrast, the need to blame someone for the ills of society is apparent in history since the beginning—the concept and its practice never die. Similarly, its theatrical counterpart is mirrored throughout time in the role of the fall guy.

One of the great ills of the world in the seventeenth century was illness itself, and along with providing playwrights an adjective with which to divine the morality of the man beneath a head of red hair, the word *dissembling* was one of the five options provided to contemporary physicians to diagnose causes of suspicious illness. The others? *Distraction, disease, doubt,* and *diabolism.*

Diabolism, the action caused by the devil, could not be perpetuated alone, or so contemporary thinking went. After entering a person—presumably one at a time—the devil would need help to spread his evil work and for this, the Old Poker relied on the demons, defined as evil spirits, to do his deeds. And, as the Elizabethan ban illustrates, witches were believed to be living freely among the populace. At one time identified individually as pagans, heathens, idolaters, witches, or heretics, these variant groups soon became associated with demons and viewed as nonbelievers—which they were not; instead they were deeply invested in their separate, centuries-old organic beliefs. They just didn't believe in Him, which is what mattered to the religious zealots of the day, who saw them all as anti-Christian devil-worshippers.

In Europe, persecution of witches had its roots in the

medieval church, where a Middle Age heretic needed to do little else to earn that sobriquet than believe something other than the church's current teaching, be warned against those beliefs, and then continue to publicize them in word or deed. In the early years of the church, punishment was light and could include forced fasting, pilgrimage, or prayer. Soon, the penalty escalated to tortue, and by the year 407, a decree placed heresy on the level of treason. Byzantine emperor Justinian (527–565) alone is believed to be responsible for approximately 100,000 executions of pagans or heretics. Perhaps the best-known purge is the Spanish Inquisition, which occurred in the fourteenth and fifteenth centuries, when European national monarchs gained control over the church. King Ferdinand and Queen Isabella fanned their country's pyres, stoking them with Jews, Muslims, and political opponents.

Rome's version of the purges swept up such luminaries as Galileo Galilei (1564–1642). The Protestant Inquisition refers to purging in the name of religious uniformity and covers events occurring in Geneva under John Calvin (1509–1564) and in England under Queen Elizabeth. Though Elizabeth was initially fairly accepting of the great schism in her country—which stemmed from the reign of her half-sister Mary—after her excommunication by the pope in 1570, she executed about two hundred Roman Catholics who ignored her declaration that it was treason to celebrate Roman Catholic Mass, join the Catholic church, or call her a heretic.

At the end of this craze came the American witch hunt. Sparsely populated and rigid in its beliefs and posture, Puritan New England had a strong acceptance of the cause of all human suffering, defining it as God's will. The sick were expected first to look inward to find the spiritual fault that caused the physical symptom. If they were righteous and good and found none, New Englanders were told that the next best thing was to look for an external force. And look they did, just as their European cousins had, searching for something that stood out, marking the ill, weak, and otherwise inexplicably odd.

Estimates are that less 4 percent of the world's population is red-haired. This means that there were at most a handful of ruddy-colored individuals in the American settlements. Amid the backdrop of a harsh life, they would surely stand out. Perhaps as much as sin itself, as is described by Edward Taylor, a well-known New England Puritan, who wrote, "My sin is red: I'm under God's arrest," borrowing the existing themes of Satan as not only the personification but also the colorization of evil.

In 1640s New England, one acceptable force that the church and citizens agreed upon was witchcraft, as evidenced by the existence of laws making witchcraft a capital offense in the colonies of Plymouth, Rhode Island, Massachusetts, Connecticut, New Haven, and New Hampshire. And in this, the young colonies mirrored some settlements around the globe, where the move from fear to law united the believers, diverse as they were, against the nonbelievers, as unruly as they appear to have been. In some parts of the world, this fear went so far as to briefly unite even Protestants and Catholics in the beliefs that Satan was actively recruiting mortals, that the miracles of the church were holy works of God, and so consequently that the potions made and healings performed by others had to be diabolical magic.

Even educated people joined in, including some physicians for whom the debate echoed the one over Judas himself—whether the devil somehow stirred up the afflicted or actually moved in and took possession of the body in question. And it may be here that a silent backstory is at the heart of how redheads ended up burning on the pyres of Europe and swinging in the nooses in America: by association. Nowhere but in hearsay can one find an edict stating that redheads are possessed of the devil and should be killed. And yet a strong belief persists that they were. I had heard it all my life. "All redheads are witches." It is something redheads are told and retell to others, and while it is evidenced, albeit slightly, in the association with pixies and their otherworldly talents, the power of this belief suggests that it must have a more primal, ancient source.

Reasonable thought could not overpower the prevailing winds of fear, and the carnage of the witch hunts was under way. The most famous of the American witch hunts took place in Salem, Massachusetts, in 1692, when two hundred people were accused, nineteen hanged, and one stoned to death. Bad as it was, it was swift in both its execution and shelf life, extinguished along with its worldwide cousin at the beginning of the 1700s, when the hard evidence of medical data became the method of determining causes of behavior and illness. Reasonable thought supplanted hysteria when a materialistic view of medicine emerged in which physical changes had symptomatic results. Dissembling and diabolism could not survive as possible stops along the way in a differential diagnosis.

In its heyday, the hatred of heresy spawned several handbooks, among them the *Malleus Maleficarum* (the Witch Hammer), published in the 1480s and popularly known as the handbook of the Inquisition. Surpassed in popularity in its time only by the Bible, it detailed the process for identifying, seeking out, and destroying witches. I searched its pages, looking among the listed classic identifying marks of a witch, to find any statement such as "All redheads are witches." None in my copy. Which reduced this hand-me-down red hair–witch connection to little more than hearsay, and at the same time suggested the fear of redheads may be based in something older than witchcraft, something understood, or implied, by the time of the Salem witch trials. A direct quote would have nailed the source, ending the search by shimmying down to the root. But it wasn't there. Instead, the continued implicit response to the powers of red hair made me marvel at its longevity.

I asked Susan Cocalis, a University of Massachusetts, Amherst, professor of Germanic languages and literature, about the "all redheads are witches" belief, to which she replied, "The red-hair witch connection is not specific to the Malleus. It has long been a folk belief in Germanic culture and has been used as a symbol of a connection to hell in literature well into the 20th century."

Understanding any solid redheaded connection to hell depends on spotting the mark of the devil, or witch mark, as it was sometimes mistakenly called; they initially existed as separate traditions but quickly got smudged into one. Reports of the devil's mark (*stigmata diaboli*) or the devil's seal (*sigillum diaboli*) are found in nearly every account of the witch trials and appear to become intertwined in their prosecutorial use. Initially, however, the devil's mark was said to be a scar, a mole, a wart, or a constellation of freckles, whereas the witch's mark was a protuberance of some kind on the body from which others were believed to suck or nurse. In writings of the sixteenth and seventeenth centuries, the devil is portrayed making compacts with witches and sealing these deals by giving them some form of identifying mark. It may be Lambert Daneau, a Calvinist theologian, who was the earliest writer to stress the interconnection between the devils and witches through these marks in his *Les sorciers*, written in 1564 and translated into English in 1575 *(A Dialogue of Witches).*

Rare as redheads were, it is possible that they merely fell in among the suspect, much as we are suspicious of anything unusual. Or it may be that when stripped, as witches nearly always were during examination—the devil believed to most frequently place his mark on the witches' most private parts—that the shocking sight of red pubic hair may have been all the brand some people needed to see to make a connection to the fires of hell. On white skin, the red hair produces an image of hot and cold, of adolescence and temptation; the sheer pinkish-white skin of redheads, whose nipples do not darken as they age and whose axillary hair does not fade from its astonishing, vibrant hue, would do nothing to temper the initial suspicions of the onlooker. The very clash of colors would confirm the suspicion that something was not right. Because naked redheads betray something, upset and undermine the idea of color we expect to find, particularly on a woman, suggesting eternal youth and adolescence as well as the sin of temptation. And in the height of times of suspicion, such as the witch trials, red hair could easily be proof enough of the belief that the devil sealed his bargain by licking witches' genitalia.

Or could it? No American or other statistics survive as to the breakdown of the physical descriptions of the condemned heretics. What does survive is the belief that having red hair marked one for the suspicion of otherworldly powers, an idea visible in the Chapman recipe for poison and the apparition of red-haired pixies.

Clearly, something more than the shock of white skin and red hair was at work, something about witches that the Elizabethan audiences implicitly responded to and that carried over from the hatred of red hair as well as from its diabolical roots. When the witch grabbed the spotlight from Shylock, an ancient theme resounded, one as old as man, one that is in our blood and has been there all along, because it is in our blood that our associations between color and character are established.

My first inkling of the primal connection between blood and character came with a pain in my thigh, a pain I have experienced nearly every moment of witch camp. It is my pentagram, one of its five points burrowing through the soft cotton pocket of my jeans. Bought when I was fourteen and worn through college, the necklace had been an essential component of my adolescent identity, as much as my long, parted-in-the-middle red hair. And though I coyly told my parents' friends that it was merely a naturalist protest symbol, what I really liked was how much it agitated older people and how very much boys my age ogled it. It hung between my teenage breasts, begging for someone to ask. And they did.

I didn't explain to young men looking into my hazel eyes that, in strictly scientific terms, the multicomposite structure of my irises makes them the most prone of the eye colors to catch surrounding environmental colors and shift to those ambient shades. Instead, deliberately misleading them into thinking my irises struck hues at my command, and sprinkling in easy references to things like witch hazel, I would add the last magical ingredient—the connection of my hair color to the occult—and try to cast a spell. A harmless spell, that of romance.

Like many of my generation's cherished teenage souvenirs, my pentagram was procured in a head shop. The place sold rolling paper and pipes and, to my utter delight, Wiccan symbols. And in my first brush with the stereotype, the round-eyed guy who clasped the silver chain around my teenaged throat said raspily, "All redheads are witches." I was thrilled. And, as he secured the necklace at the back, I was hooked. What followed was a membership in a monthly occult book club, though the powers I chose to explore were limited to those of intimate persuasion. I never stuck pins in anything, attended a coven, or corresponded with other witches, but I wore the pentagram everywhere, never realizing that in its upside-down position, it represents the powers of black magic. Three decades later, moments before departing for camp found me polishing up my pentagram and shoving it into my jeans, which is where it would remain. At camp the symbol is everywhere: hanging from ears, around necks on chains, through noses and navels. Mary Elizabeth deftly points out that the pentagram on every other witch is pointing upward. Mine, I realize, needs to stay in my pocket. And it does, as I crouch in a circle, at class.

At the opening of witch camp there were courses of study to select. As acknowledged entry-level campers, Mary Elizabeth and I surveyed the choices and chose a course titled "Path," which is pretty much Witchcraft 101, a study of the elements: earth, air, fire, water, and the spirit. Though we were not disappointed to find that none of the courses taught how to render the fat of a redhead, we were somewhat surprised that there was no practical magic being taught. And no black magic, whatsoever.

Our Path course is being run by a man who is wearing a skirt and a baseball cap and carrying a banjo. And in that he would be easy to dismiss were he not also wearing a T-shirt advertising Element, a skateboard company, supplying a bemusing balance between the pagan world and those outside it.

We begin today's session with air. He invokes the wind and begins chanting, "Breath, breeze, gale, hurricane. Powers to begin. Breath, breeze, air, hurricane. Powers of the wind. Air, I am calling you. Air, I am calling you. Air, I am calling you. Powers to begin." It all seems harmless enough. The purpose, he tells us, is to go singly through the elements each day of this week, seeking unlikely experiences with each, all in the name of fulfilling our potential. In this we are connecting to the outer world, and as we do so, it certainly feels as though we have lost touch with the here and now. Huddled around a small fire in an open-air wooden shelter, we are performing an ancient rite, following a leader in a seamless organic ritual in which the spiritual is an unseen entity outside ourselves—in this case, the wind.

The witch reminds us that the elements are portrayed in the pentagram and that to understand the connection of the elements, we must draw a pentagram without raising the pencil from the paper, connecting its five points without a break. Elongate the regular sides of a pentagon until they meet and you'll have a pentagram, an occult symbol used by Pythagoreans and later by philosophers and magicians. Also referred to as a pentacle or pentangle, the pentagram has associations with the five fingers of the hand, the five senses, the head and four limbs of man and woman, and especially, the elements—the spirit at the top of the upward facing point, followed to the right by water, fire, earth, and air. When drawn, the five points are connected in order of density—from top to lower right, to upper left, across to upper right, down to lower left and up again—in the order of spirit, fire, air, water and earth, their connection being essential to the understanding of their power.

The presence of the elements in this pagan setting bridges thousands of years and connects several continents of human history, specifically through healing. Though when attempting to overlay the predominant schemas of medicine at work in the world today—Eastern, as represented primarily by Chinese medicinal values; Indian, as represented in the Ayurvedic traditions; and Western, as represented in the emphasis on healing versus prevention—the task is made simpler by looking only to the traditions' similarities and avoiding their enormous differences. In the beginning of each was an acceptance of the elements and the need to bring their polar opposites into balance. In traditional Chinese medicine these elements are fire, earth, metal, water, and wood. The Ayurvedic tradition combines the five elements of the universe in specific ways to form three unique doshas, or skin/body types of a person: Vata, Pitta, and Kapha. Within each of us, it is believed that there are seven chakras, or nodes of energy, two of which are located in the head and five in the body, and it is those five that are also associated with the five elements. At the ancient root of Western medicine is a belief in four elements of which all matter is composed—earth, water, air, and fire—which, in turn, correspond to what became known as the four humors.

The theory of the four humors is elaborate, in its time influencing popular thought about medicine, character, and personality and providing a strong method of interpreting oneself. Grounded in the idea of fifth-century Sicilian philosopher Empedocles that all matter is made up of one or more of the four basic elements, the theory has natural counterparts in the four bodily fluids as well as in the four seasons of the year.

The humors are perhaps best read in a volume published at a time in which they were widely examined and applied— as opposed to now, when they suffer mightily from being painted with the New Age brush of passionate inaccuracy. There is no better reference than the gargantuan text *The Anatomy of Melancholy*, which at its first publication in 1621 was a huge success and was followed by five subsequent editions by its author, Robert Burton (1577–1640). There is also no better book in which to explore how the pagan measures against the pious; how what each believes conflicts as well as intersects in their separate attempts to explain just what it is that ails man.

Simply put, earth, water, air, and fire correspond to qualities of dry, wet, cold, and hot, each of which is associated with one of the four fluid—and colored—substances of the body; black bile, phlegm, blood, and yellow bile. These, in turn, are associated with autumn, winter, spring, and summer and the qualities of melancholic, phlegmatic, sanguine, and choleric, which must be in harmony or balance. Otherwise, one runs the risk of becoming too melancholic, phlegmatic, sanguine, or choleric and must be treated by its opposite regimen to restore the condition of health.

These also developed temperament associations, later

known as temperament theory, in which all of humankind is divided into predispositions toward being either the melancholic type; the phlegmatic, or sluggish, type; the sanguine, or zesty, type; or the choleric, or quick-tempered, type.

Matching these behavioral models are four fundamental color energies representing each person's behavior, style, health, and desires. It is simple to see that I am red both in hair color and in complexion. Typing me by this single trait, I would have thought my association would be to fire. It's not; it's to air, too much of which makes one sanguine, the color of blood, associated with spring and a passionate disposition. And with a mock gasp of recognition, I find myself easily here: I'm red-haired, born in spring under the sign of Mars (the Red Planet), and passionate. These things are true. Too simple, of course, though they happen to line up with the humors, from color to season to disposition. But the tight fit could influence me to apply this handy ancient palette to understanding others, as well. It's familiar, after all, especially if you've ever been happy in the spring, or depressed in the fall. Familiar, too, after reading about Cain, Esau, David, Judas, and Shylock. And familiar to anyone looking for wisdom outside Western tradition and in the world's other predominant healing traditions: In traditional Chinese medicine, excessive redness in the complexion is due to excessive heat caused by a predominance of yang and deficiency of yin. In Ayurvedic medicine, the first, or root, chakra is associated with the color red, the element of the earth and the promise that, after getting this chakra into balance, one might be better able to control one's emotions. At the heart of all three major medicinal schemas is the primary association of the color red with blood.

Greek medicine taught that good health depended on balancing the humors, which later led to the practices of purging the digestive tract and draining the blood. For the latter, you went to a barber. At least you did after A.D. 1163, following a church edict stating that you must. A relic of that remains with us today in the red and white barber pole, a holdover from a time when it advertised the services of someone who was both barber and bloodletter. And so medicine remained for centuries, although blood became considered the paramount humor, literally the bearer of life. Red, and thicker than water, blood has always colored the way people think. In some ancient springtime festivals, the color red seen in the mud-filled, fast-running streams in that season was strongly associated with the blood of lost heroes. Modern usage of the word *sanguine*, for instance, reveals ancient associations, intertwining the personality traits of being "cheerfully optimistic," in its first definition; having a ruddy complexion, in its second and followed by simply being "bloody," whose derivative is *sanguinary*, meaning "bloodthirsty."

The pursuit of defining character traits along lines of color can be traced back to a book attributed to Aristotle, and entitled *Physiognomics*, probably written in the third century B.C.E. and included in his *Minor Works*. "Those with tawny colored hair are brave; witness the lions," the author wrote. "The reddish are of bad character; witness the foxes."

The pseudoscience of physiognomics thrust upon the public the idea of interpreting human character, intelligence, and virtue through the analysis of physical appearances. A hot topic for the Greeks, it was what Chaucer was depending on us understanding when, in his fourteenth-century *Canterbury Tales*, the loud, uncouth miller appears in his red beard, "like any sow or fox," his nose sporting a tuft of red hair "red as the bristles in an old sow's ear." By Chaucer's time, thanks in part to the physiognomic writings of the day, red hair was fixed in its meaning.

How we now respond to red-haired men seems baseless until it is examined in light of these historic precedents. Think for a moment about any red-haired man. When you do, you use very different language than you would if you were thinking about a red-haired woman. When we say "redhead," we invariably mean a woman. If it's a man, the language changes to "he's got red hair," or "that guy with red hair." Think of famous redheaded males. Consider Thomas Jefferson, Red Skelton, and Woody Woodpecker; none of them bubble up in the consciousness in quite the same way as do Rita and Lucy. Whisper "redhead" to yourself and the Rolodex of the mind flips to women; softly form the phrase "red-headed guy," and what is thrown up is Opie Taylor, Alfred E. Neuman, and Howdy Doody. Or, worse, Archie. Worst of all: Bozo the Clown. The historic reaction to the red-haired man was a kind of loathing, which is not all that astonishing when considered under the shadow cast by Shylock's red wig and its dual message of fear and amused derision. Similarly, the enormous degree to which our fearful perception of the red-haired man has waned is tied solely to this idea of slighted humor, which eventually brought us this view we have of red-haired men as diminished beings, lesser to other men and certainly less powerful than their female counterparts.

When red-haired women take on the role of clown, as Lucille Ball did in her early *I Love Lucy* television persona, they are tredding on the middle ground, turf they may share with the red-haired male. When they take on the comic identity, however, the lesser of the two evils associated with red-haired men, female redheads lose something in the bargain. The comic role instantly diminishes their aura of being highly sexualized. Because clowns are not sexy.

Lacking the role of jester, the red-haired female plays her primal role, that of desire, specifically, the one who is in its control. Then she is Lilith and Eve or, more to the point, she is what is brewed when the devil colludes with Lilith, and then Lilith entices Eve, creating a laying on of hands that beckons men toward sin. And it is in her primal role that the red-haired woman is at her most powerful. After all, what could be more of a temptation to man than the daughter of the devil himself?

Humors to blood. Blood to foxes. Foxes to sex. The sexes divide. Can it be that simple? When Aristotle identified red hair as being explicitly like foxes, did that set a course of implicit eternal distrust of redheads? It might have, depending on how one looked at the fox.

In many traditions the fox appears as a symbol of cunning and trickery, the origin of which appears to be its red color (though not all foxes are red, of course), which, in turn, places it among the devil's followers. The fox, who is also associated with both Set and Thor, is also linked with witches, in its ability to mislead humans, as in being dissembling, as well as in the method for its ritual extermination, burning. Witches were burned because it was considered un-Christian to shed their blood. In some ritual burnings, the ashes of foxes, like those of Set, were scattered. Also, like witches, foxes are thought to be highly sexual. Like red-haired men, foxes became an ingredient in a potion, though in the animals' case it was their testicles that were ground up and added to wine as an aphrodisiac in ancient China, where foxtails were also known to be worn on the arm as a form of arousal. In Hans Biedermann's *Dictionary of Symbolism, Cultural Icons and the Meanings Behind Them,* in China, female spirits rode on foxes and were said to be "incredibly seductive, and their unbridled sexual demands can steal the life-force of men who succumb to them."

What you believe about a fox may be that it is red, close to the ground, and skillful. What you believe *in* is different and may include the production of potions, the wearing of foxtails, and other forms of sympathetic magic to utilize and transport the powers of the fox. Bridging the things we believe and those we believe in is done in myriad systems of superstitions. Consider offering a blessing to someone who sneezes. Despite knowing that sneezes have biological origins, you still offer a "God bless you," and in doing so, connect back to a time when it was roundly believed that the devil entered the body however he could—the open mouth was an efficient conveyance, for example.

And it is in how he enters us that the devil gets what he is after. In the case of red hair on women, evidence suggests strong, historic belief in the devil's ability to enter women and infuse them with the ultimate power of desire. And he does so in the fluid of the paramount humor, our blood. But not just any blood; rather, that primal, confusing blood that divides the boys from the girls and the girls from the women and that has always upset us so—menstrual blood.

Menstrual blood scares us. In the case of redheads, it is believed to scare the hell into us.

Perhaps back to the beginning of man, and certainly exhibited worldwide, there have been fears, taboos, and even laws about how women are to conduct themselves when menstruating. According to Dr. Dawn Starin, an anthropologist and a research associate at the University College London, over time and across cultures the rules about menstruation basically break down to either restricting society from "the destructive forces" of menstruating women or "protect the menstruating woman from society." When it comes to the fear menstruation inspires, at its heart the monthly blood represents a woman's failure to conceive—which conversely, and from the beginning of time, according to Starin, could be taken to be an insult upon man, "a bloodletting that brutally denied his new role as child-maker." And while feminist writers argue that taboos against menstruating women are little more—or less—than signs of the male dominance of society, Starin cites the root of these taboos as the centuries-old belief that mating with a menstruating woman is "evil and dangerous" and "the devil's work."

Starin is not alone in her menstruation research. It is a topic that is widely covered in the 1922 classic *The Golden Bough*, in which the author James George Frazer discusses the taboo as well as the varying ways in which women in history have been secluded during their monthly periods.

"Ancient Greeks, Romans, Hebrews, Christians, Muslims, Chinese, Hindus and almost every other group considered a menstruating woman unclean," Starin wrote in a 2004 paper titled "Bloody Red Heads." Those who broke the prescription and had sexual intercourse during menstruation were "parents with no self-control," and their offspring were marked for life. Among the marks of the devil were syphilis, gonorrhea, leprosy, birthmarks, freckles, and—of course—red hair.

Fraught with misconception, based in fear and ignorance, the strong beliefs in every culture about the monthly blood of women run the spectrum from the failure of a man to impregnate a woman to, at their least onerous end, the strong association with impurity. Even the seemingly timid contemporary version of baptism is deeply rooted in the washing away of the birthing blood, a form of bleeding that confused the early church, having both a sexual association (if a woman was really pure, she'd make like the Virgin Mary and do without sex) and a link to the gift of life. And I'd seen it myself, once coming right up against a contemporary belief arising from the fear of female bleeding in the words of a buxom fundamentalist.

Just a few days after the second of my two miscarriages, I was at an office holiday party with my husband. At the time, he was working with a man whose fundamental Christianity infused his daily work routine. The man would ask people to openly pray with him for business success and to witness their faith. My husband is good in these situations, so much so that we have a deal: I make war and he makes peace. We both come by these traits by heredity: His father was a minister; mine a sportswriter. So he never prayed with that coworker, but with my husband's innate grace, no one got socked in the eye.

At the party, the wife of the man who liked to pray at work came wafting across the room toward me in a white dress with strategic sequin-limned cutouts playing peekaboo over her substantial cleavage. Sinking to her knees, her dress collapsing like a half-baked angel food cake, she placed those cutouts right in my line of vision.

"I have been praying for you," she said. And I thanked her and tried to get her up off the ground by starting to raise myself above her breast level. But she stayed and I slunk back down.

She took both of my hands and placed my palms together, sandwiched within hers.

Then she told me to pray, saying that it was my only defense against Satan, and in that she infuriated me, suggesting I could do more, that my behavior left me open to succumbing to another miscarriage. It must have shown in my eyes because her entreaties to pray became more urgent. And then she clarified her point for me: "It's the devil who takes pregnancies, you know," she said. I knew that only biology could explain the miscarriage. And now I know that the only explanation for this ridiculous woman was thousands of years of fear and loathing that had lodged themselves into her in the form of this leftover scrap of a notion. Picked apart, she surely would not have been able to trace its origin, but she had absorbed what she needed, leaving the rest of it behind. Part of what she was alluding to was true, of course—that part that reminds us that the fear of the devil's power has deep red roots in our blood and that the desire we feel for red-haired women is rooted there, as well. But in today's terms, the fundamentalist's beliefs about my inability to carry a pregnancy to term appear to be nothing more than superstition, an idea or notion not based on reason or logic.

I admit it: My first response was to think of that woman as one ignorant bitch. But that is about as informed a response as was hers; not much is learned in either. She didn't know what she was talking about, that's true. She could not have identified the historic links to blood in her superstitions, but that is because they are implicit, under-ground, and quiet. In this, her response to my miscarriage mirrors those reactions that redheaded men and women encounter all the time. Ask someone why they think red-heads are fiery, sexual, or distrustful. They won't quite know the answer. But chances are good they believe these ideas to be true.

Part of the reason for both the lack of connection to our superstitions and our continued attachment to them is that superstitions appear singular of purpose. Not walking under a ladder seems utterly unrelated to not taking the last cookie from the plate for fear of becoming an old maid. In this age, if we think of superstitions at all, it is more with the affection we apply to our bumper stickers than with any consideration we give to related sets of incorporated beliefs. Superstitions are simple to apply. Historically, however, superstitions are preventive measures and are not without connection to one another. They are systems through which we were both instructed and controlled. They are instant in their accessibility—don't step on a crack!—as well as casual about their source material, and most people neither ques-tion them nor trace them to their origins. In this, they require less of our consideration than do religion or science. Slapped onto our fear of the unknown, superstitions allow us to move swiftly through the darkness by providing reassurance as well as rules to live by, silly though some of them may seem.

My grandfather, a native of Liverpool, taught me that among the Victorian riggers and men who worked along the docks of that great city, a widespread belief was that meeting a redhead at the beginning of a journey was a terrible thing. Coming upon one while still on the dock or even already onboard ship, the beholder was supposed to return home. Born in 1881, this same grandfather had a curious habit of standing in an open doorway at exactly midnight as New Year's Eve turned into New Year's Day.

Without knowing its meaning, I had steadfastly continued this habit all my life, shivering in every doorway I've rented or owned since it was first taught to me, teaching it to my husband, and these days letting our young daughter stay up late only this one night of the year to do the same. Figuring it was time to understand my own behavior, I went looking for the ritual's meaning.

Our doorway tradition is a variation of Hogmanay, when, in both English and Scottish tradition, we let out the old year and let in the new. This tradition has pagan origins in the belief that it is the spirits of those years who are being allowed to flow in as well as out of the house.

The connection to redheads is found in the superstitions about the color of the hair of the person whose foot first crosses your threshold in the New Year, and it was a scholar in Great Britain who offered me that explanation. Professor Ronald Hutton, of the Department of Historical Studies at the University of Bristol, wrote: "Redheads were generally thought unlucky as the first callers at New Year, in the zone of northern England and southern Scotland where 'first-footing' customs were important during the past three hundred years."

Evil, betrayer, someone to be avoided right from the very first day of the year, redheaded men and women are viewed in many cultures as the last person you want to be first over your New Year threshold, as evidenced by the bad luck that will inevitably follow. Regardless of their sex, the belief held that a dark-haired person brought the best luck, a blond meant no luck at all, a widower bad luck, and a redhead the worst luck possible. Thus began a tradition among those who could afford it, of hiring first-footers, as they came to be known, to cross first.

According to Hutton, "Local tradition was, however, variable, and in a few communities red hair was actually the most desirable in a first caller."

And yet my grandfather married a tall redhead, perhaps illustrating Professor Hutton's sense of the desirability of the hair color in some communities. When I mentioned that possibility to New York folklorist Dr. Ellen Damsky, who describes herself as an "almost former redhead," she related: "I remember ballad scholar David Buchan asking politely that I not show up at his house too early on New Year's Day—apparently if a redhead is the first to cross over the threshold (Scottish/Irish belief?), bad luck follows into the New Year."

According to Dr. Yvonne Milspaw, an Indiana University folklorist, not only is red hair suspect, but also its attendant freckles are ominous and should be removed. Here, according to Milspaw, is one method for doing so that survives in the folklore: "Early in the morning on May Day, kneel in the wet grass, wipe dew on your hands, across your face and then on your butt [unspecified but implied—a bare butt]. Freckles will be transferred from your face to your butt."

And if you are not out naked in the morning dew, perhaps it is because you are in jail, locked up on account of your typical redheaded behavior and the trouble it got you in the night before. Or so thought an Irish judge in 2001, who, while passing sentence, told the defendant that his fiery temper was caused by his red hair. "I am a firm believer that hair colouring has an effect on temper," she told him for the record, "and your colouring suggests you have a temper." She then fined him for disorderly conduct.

Even in our unconscious the implicit themes of hair imagery thrive, according to Sigmund Freud. He believed that castration presents itself thematically in our dreams in images of balding, or of simply getting a haircut. And his theories sparked a spectrum of dream interpretation in which graying hair, for instance, may foretell contagion in the family and the cutting of hair speaks to serious disappointment. Red hair is said to presage change, so much so that if you are a man and dream your lover is a redhead, we are told, your near future will bring accusations of unfaithfulness by that lover.

Proverbs are another method of expressing common-place truths. Short and popular, they are usually untraceable in origin, though effective in their expression of fear and how to manage that fear. "A red beard and a black head, catch him with good trick and take him dead" is an Old English proverb about red hair. So is the warning to say your prayers when meeting a red-haired man, since he is not to be trusted. A French proverb reminds us, "Red-headed women are either violent or false, and usually are both."

Anthropologist Dawn Starin notes that redheaded children, believed to be products of unclean sex, have historically been called "red-knob" in Champagne and "Griserli blunt" (horribly blond) in Alsace, and in some English-speaking countries, they continue to be referred to as "tampon tops." According to Dr. Starin, a European children's rhyme exists to this day that states, "You red one, jump over the wall, break your neck and legs, never come home alive."

Irish folklore and music is full of red-hair references, not all of them complimentary. Take for example, "Red Haired Mary," a popular song by Sean McCarthy, whose lyrics vary slightly from singer to singer but whose theme and message remain fixed. Right from the first line—"While going to the fair of Dingle"—the listener is clued to the evil portent of the tale, for folklore states that nothing but bad luck will come of meeting a red-haired girl on the way to the fair and, like meeting one on the docks or onboard, that the viewer should turn right around and go home. In this case, however, the fairgoer spots a red-haired girl named Mary and takes no heed, instead inviting her to ride with him on his donkey. As he's bidding her farewell, the narrator relates in the third stanza, "A tinker man stepped up beside me, and he belted me in the eye." The man who threw the punch, we learn, was scheduled to marry the girl that morning, but she then throws him over, offering to her ride to "forget the priest this morning and tonight we'll lie in Murphy's shed."

The jilted tinker in the song relates to tinkers, these days known as Irish travelers, or "itinerants," a much disliked tiny minority in Ireland, England and the United States, who previously lived and traveled in caravans begging and mending pots. Sometimes wrongly confused with Gypsies, they speak their own language, Shelta, and in previous generations held occupations as tinsmiths, thus their name. These days the term "tinker" is derogatory, though still used, indicating the rough habits and migrant ways of a population said to be mostly red-haired.

This theme is repeated in "The Tinkerman's Daughter," a ballad in which a farmer spots a tinkers' camp and in it, the beautiful red-haired Ann, whose father sells the girl the next day for the price of a pony and who, for her part, behaves as the color apparently dictates, and leaves their bed one night never to return.

Some of the Irish bad feelings about red hair can be traced to a historic fear of the Vikings who, even in popular culture, continue to be thought of as raping, pillaging madmen. Some of them were, of course, but not all. All of them had other nonvoyaging tasks, something to do once they got where they were going and settled down. Mostly, that was farming, meaning that some people were only seasonal Vikings, going off "a-viking" (lowercase, mostly meaning pirating), when the weather turned warm. Any Viking was a seafaring, shipbuilding person, part of a group that had its heyday for approximately three hundred years (approximately C.E. 800 to 1100). During that time they traveled by sea, ranging more than five thousand miles from Persia to the New World across the Atlantic.

The English term "Viking" is derived from the Old Norse word *vikinger*, which probably comes from *vik*, or "bay," making its people bay men who skulked along the coasts and then attacked. They were the last of the Germanic barbarian conquerors and they were the first of the seafaring European explorers. But they were not one people. They were the Danish Vikings, who conquered England; the Norwegian Vikings, who moved into Scotland and Ireland as well as the North Atlantic Islands and, for a brief period, the coast of North America; and the Swedish Vikings, who took over the eastern Baltic. Some of them raped and pillaged and, as a result, left behind the vestiges of that behavior in both their genes and in the fear and loathing of marauding men. As a whole, the Vikings pretty much settled down and were absorbed into the indigenous population, making a distinctive impression in the look, language, and culture of those places. This is particularly true in England's Lancashire County, home of Southport and Liverpool, where the Norse yielded such place names ending in "kirk," as in Ormskirk, where Margaret Pilkington, my English grandmother, was born, and in "dale," as in Birkdale, where she lived as a child. Despite popular misconception, not all Vikings were red-haired, though most were light in both hair and skin color and many were redheads.

It is through the Vikings that we get a word whose two syllables encase the enormous, enduring fear we associate with them. The word is *berserk*, which, at some point between 1865 and 1870, began its English language usage as an adjective. Coming from an ancient Scandinavian legend, *berserk* describes a Norse warrior who fought with frenzied rage in battle. Combining the word for "bear" with that for "shirt," it describes what the marauders were seen to be wearing: fur. *Norse* is a term that pertains to ancient Scandinavia. Only some Scandinavians were Vikings, but the Vikings as a whole have never really recovered from this association as berserkers.

Another example of a single word harboring a powerful, red-haired history is that of *ruffian*, a tidy little noun that carries in it ancient, unheard themes that subtly sway the senses and influence our response. Connoting a swaggering bully, *ruffian* entered the English language in the sixteenth century, with connections to the word *ruffle*, its noun being *ruffler* (as in one who disturbs, vexes, or irritates). Earlier derivation associates a ruffian with the Latin word *rufus*, or "red," as well as connecting it to the *ruffiani*, or Roman pimps, who offered the *services meretrices*, or female prostitutes, on the street. The hair color of the Roman whores was usually either red or golden blond, to differentiate them from the nonworking girls of the local population. Looking in literature, the *ruffiani* can be found with other malicious purveyors of fraud, in the eighth level of hell, as designated in Dante Aligheri's *Divine Comedy*. The last, or ninth, ring was reserved for the betrayers of God, Judas among them.

Some of the bad feeling about red hair shows up as more than a single word and less than a proverb. These are expressions or simple beliefs. A Russian tradition holds that red hair is not only the sign of a fiery temper but also that in calling someone a redhead you are saying he or she is crazy. In contemporary Singapore, the quirky slang, Singlish, in which English follows Chinese grammar, is peppered with words from Indian and Malay dialects, including sarong party girl, or SPG, meaning a woman who hangs out with male ang moh—literally meaning red-haired, which is used to describe anyone Caucasian.

Things are no better on the island on which the greatest concentration of redheads thrives. In the United Kingdom, redheads sometimes refer to themselves as "copperknobs," "carrot tops," and members of the "Ginger Nation." Dr. Starin relates much of this to the menstrual blood fear, citing even the playground insult that "redheads stink," as being rooted in the mistaken belief that menstruating women smell bad.

On the smell of red-haired women, I had only read one thing and it was charming. According to French writer Augustin Galopin, whose book *Le parfum de la femme* was published in Paris in 1886, he can detect a woman's hair color by her smell, blonds being the most faintly scented, brunettes next in line, and redheads having the strongest scent. Redheads and women with chestnut hair smell of amber or of violets, he wrote, while brunettes have the scent of ebony, and blonds, copying redheads, carry the aroma of amber or violets but in a degree that is much more subtle.

That lovely ideal doesn't seem to pervade literature, since there are far more references to the problems with redheads than to the joys. Dr. Starin cites the prejudice in Central Africa's Cameroon, where red-haired albinos, known as Nguenguerous, are believed to have come by their physical condition "after their mothers had sexual relations during their menstrual periods." Prejudice against albinos in Chad, Gabon, and Congo has resulted in groups advocating for their rights. From time to time, various world organizations including the United Nations have made efforts to study the allegations of that discrimination, some of which include charges of ritual murder.

Even modern medicine perpetuates a connection between red hair and menstruation, as seen in the Ayurvedic belief that anyone with red hair has a large amount of the dosha Pitta and that the inherent medical conditions of redheads include excessive sweating and long, heavy menstrual periods. Nor is Western medicine immune to such notions. A dentist once told me that all redheads bleed more during surgery. More recently, an orthopedic surgeon revealed that he had a partner who believed that "if anything can go wrong in surgery, it will go wrong with a redhead." During an office visit later with that partner, the man admitted to me that while he believes the idea to be true, he would not be quoted by name. It "just sounds too crazy," he said.

Negative stereotyping of red hair in England is reported in such mainstays of the mainstream media as the *Guardian* newspaper, *BBC News*, and the *Daily Express*. Peppered with features about charges of discrimination of red-haired individuals, news accounts include one recent round of insults hurled over a power company ad campaign whose photos featured redheads—including one man looking sadly down into his underpants—and whose slogan reads, "There are some things in life you can't choose."

We would never portray a redheaded woman that way, of course. Watching her look into her pants we wouldn't be pondering shame. No doubt about it. It would be sex that was on our minds.

Even some scientific studies of redheads have done nothing to dispel these notions, rather simply recording them and offering them as data. Under the heading "Redheads and Blonds: Stereotypic Images," a 1986 *Psychological Reports* article makes the claim that "hair-color stereotypes seem to be very long-lasting and robust," and goes on to report the perception that blond females are "beautiful, pleasant and extremely feminine," and blond males "strong, active, pleasant, successful, and good-looking." Redheaded females, the study maintains, are viewed by the public as "unattractive but competent and professional," as well as "rugged, complex, colorful, and strong willed."

Redheaded males, however, are seen as "unattractive, less successful and rather effeminate" and were not viewed by anyone other than other redheaded males to be "superior in any trait." The older the respondent, however, the more redheaded women gained in status. Not so for redheaded men, who, as the interviewees aged, were increasingly viewed as "sad, effeminate, unpleasant, weak, slow and shallow," and displaying the phenotypes of "poor health."

Much of that is absurd, as are the instantaneous perceptions we make of others that are actually fueled by the numberless points of information our individual experience has allowed: We think they are made in a split second when vast influences actually have forged each. But then reality balances the perception: Knowing a redhead fulfills some stereotypes and abolishes others. In this, the beauty of red hair is in both the eye of the beholder and the hip pocket of world history. There is no viewing the identity of one without peering down into the other and both can be seen in literature.

Along with what a reader learns about red hair from Chaucer, Shakespeare, Dryden, and Chapman, a careful reader can plot a point-to-point line through the existing hellish literary references to red hair into the nineteenth and twentieth centuries. We find Charles Dickens, whose *Oliver Twist* brings us Fagin, "whose villainous-looking and repulsive face was obscured by a quantity of matted red hair." Even in *Oliver!*, the 1968 Academy Award–winning movie version, the keeper of the coins and children is portrayed with red hair and a long hanging nose, bearing the mark of Satan. Dickens also crafted the unendingly hypocritical, though "humble" red-haired Uriah Heep, in *David Copperfield*, whose countenance and character speak of no good coming to anyone. Certainly they are two of the most repugnant characters ever created, both drawing on as well as perpetuating the fear of men of a certain color. Red hair as a literary device not only had power—it has legs, moving into the twentieth century in such company as *Ulysses*, in which James Joyce employs Buck Mulligan to inform us, "Redheaded women buck like goats," which does little to dispel the belief that we are responsive in bed.

A later work than that of Joyce depends on readers' innate understanding of physiognomy. The very title of

William Golding's 1954 classic, *Lord of the Flies*, harkens back thousands of years to Beelzebub, derived from *Baalzebub*, which in Hebrew means "Lord of the Flies." In Greco-Roman times the name was used for the demons who opposed God. Christians associate Beelzebub with Satan based on passages in the Gospel of Matthew, among others. Golding's novel uses the effective device of red hair to plot the book's driving motif that man is basically evil. Marooning a mixture of choir school boys and private school boys on an island, he depicts Ralph, the first leader of the group, as blond and mostly good, with an occasional fall from grace into the evil will of the mob, including when he joins in to kill another boy. The epitome of evil, however, is Jack, the redhead in the black cloak. He breaks from the group, baptizes himself in the blood of the slaughtered pig, and forms a separate band of boys intent on hunting and savagery. The redhead's presence eventually results in Ralph being turned out on his own in the forest, and as he is, he evokes the classic role of the scapegoat.

In the twenty-first century, our fastest-growing delivery system for information is the Internet, though from it we get only as much accuracy as we do hyperbole, both delivered with astonishing speed. After typing "red hair" into an Internet search engine, the biggest hits still produce listings such "red hot XXX redheads," continuing the tradition of delivering us the temptation aspects of the hair color. Although recently I have noticed a change. The sex sites have been displaced, moved down, in the time it took to research this book. And interestingly, what now appears on top, as the first hits, are the sites regarding science. As it should be. Because to understand the history of the world of red hair, we must pack up and leave witch camp, and, as best we can, put aside folklore and expressions, superstition and myth. Though we will not be leaving blood behind. To the contrary, we need to travel deeper into its paramount secrets in order to fully identify the redhead.

PART TWO

SCIENCE

Digestif

Recipe for an Identity

I COLLECT RECIPE BOXES, the kind with handwritten index cards filed with dividers. I never buy them at yard sales or take them at random, preferring to think that my passion for the files is slightly more complex than the thrill of acquisition, that it has to do with passing on something of value: Perhaps the very ingredients of the lives lived and shared are there amid the garnish and the flour. The collection includes those of my grandmother and my husband's mother, one his mother made for him to take to college and one that belonged to his late sister, one put together by my mother's best friend, Janet, and one Janet had gotten from her mother, Hellie. There is not one from my mother. My redheaded father cooked, as did his British father, who lived with us, but they wrote none of it down.

If flipped through only archaeologically the recipes unearth what was made at the hands of these good women.

Viewed geographically, they link our family's ancestral nourishment from South Dakota, New York, and Indiana to England, Scotland, and Germany. They reveal who I am, who I became when I married, and who I am not, lacking, as they do, any recipes from Africa or Asia. That is, unless you consider my mother-in-law's Spam Chop Suey to be in any way Eastern, which would be a serious stretch for this recipe. Its four basic ingredients are Spam, fat, rice, and a can of cream of mushroom soup.

My mother-in-law's name was Lillian. Her box is unique in the collection, in that the lineage of each recipe is included, annotated with proper names: "Luella's Persimmon Pudding," "Iona's Date Pudding," "Adina's 3-Bean Salad." Everything is credited to the hand that passed it along, from Barbara Owen's popcorn balls to Paul Evans's T-shirt method of roasting a turkey ("dip T-shirt in melted butter and drape over the stuffed turkey"). While most are accompanied by hand-scribbled reviews—"Delicious!" "Great!" "Rex's favorite!"—Mary Landstrom's "delicious Cheese Squares" come with the warning, "Don't give out!" I won't.

Looked at by their recipe ingredients alone, each of the boxes I've collected may be viewed as a steady diet for sustenance, disease, or some uneasy prandial existence in between. But in their larger sense they are an inheritance. Much like my father's red hair, as well as the slender knees that he passed along to me, they speak not only of what is passed along, but also how. And in that, they speak of who we are—first of a family and then, in the hands of an individual cook, they tell us of that cook in very specific terms. They speak of his or her identity. And in this, they make a handy way to explain genetics.

In the last years of the twentieth century and the first of this one, we overturned much about how we think of who we are. And if we haven't, we should, blessed as we are now with a new appliance enabling us to examine our individual as well as human identity: genetics. Who wouldn't want a peek at what hurtles back in time way before writing and storytelling, hand tools and images scratched on a cave wall? Why let the Bible, ancient fears, schoolyard slurs, old stories of red-haired Egyptian maniacal gods, and the withering looks of fundamentalists identify us when you can strap on a clean apron and have a look at your very own ingredients?

And they are ingredients, in many ways like those in an angel food cake, or that cauldron of poison into which the fat of a red-haired man was plopped. Precise in the required amounts, each ingredient changes the others to some degree and all give the recipe its identity. Working backward from what we know now, it is safe to say that there can be no true understanding of our identity in this day and age without having a look at our genetic makeup, because it is here, in the specific combination of those ingredients, that each of us is unique; colored though we may be by rumor and story, we are each genetically our very own selves.

Let's say that the human genome is my mother-in-law Lillian's recipe file. Imagine there are twenty-three little colored tabs sticking up within it—beef, poultry, cheese, casseroles, hors d'oeuvres, etc.—and picture those as the twenty-three chromosomes in the human body. Within each of these chromosomes are genes, or, in this case, recipes—including, of course, Spam Chop Suey, with its four basic ingredients: Spam, fat, rice and a can of cream of mushroom soup. Each recipe in her box, it seems, includes some combination of these four.

The human genome equivalent of these ingredients are adenine, guanine, thymine, and cytosine written in genetic transcription as A, G, T, and C, and just like Lillian's four staples, these four are always present in every recipe.

The old-fashioned idea of the recipe box—index cards neatly in place, always at the ready—works well here too, especially when compared to how I exchange recipes. I e-mail them, particularly to my friend Elizabeth in Maine. Both of us have husbands who don't cook, daughters who are small, and budgets. And both of us inherited an uneasy sense of culinary childhood as being catch-as-catch-can, where youngsters retrieved olives from warming cocktail glasses and called them vegetables. We both hoped to not pass this on to our daughters.

Back and forth between us travels a fluent battery of recipes that get saved in a file. They go out to anyone who requests a recipe at a dinner party: The beet and ginger soup regularly leaves here electronically; the shallot pudding has been sent all over America. Ready to go with the touch of a file attachment button, these recipes are cloned without sweat—never changed, not ever reread, just attached to the e-mail that accompanies them.

By contrast, my mother-in-law's recipes are sheltered in the box that has always housed them. All written by hand or typed, they were copied over and over for her children, her friends, her fellow parishioners, sometimes with typos or edits, little mutations that may or may not survive, depending on whether they enhance (more Spam?) or dilute (more cream of mushroom soup?) the recipe, but always with the same four basic ingredients in varying weights and measures.

I have the box she made for her youngest child, my husband, and I've studied how the recipes differ from her master collection, as she adapted them to suit the appetites and kitchen skills of the college-bound boy. In his box, the chop suey recipe was reduced to a serving for one; in her large-box version, for church suppers, I have what it takes to make it *for twenty*. This is pretty much what goes on in the genetic process called replication, in which the gene is copied and passed along.

Specifically what gets passed along are known in genetics as alleles, or contrasting genes for the same trait—tall and short, for instance—one of which will predominate, much like a version of a dish that identifies a family tradition.

When we married, my husband brought his mother's recipe boxes into our home and I brought mine. For the big stuff, like Thanksgiving, we undergo what genetics calls recombination, when we shuffle and unite our two families' inherited holiday recipes and lay it out as a single feast before our unsuspecting child, who will grow up thinking that this, including Spam Chop Suey (in which I've altered every ingredient but the crunchy noodles), is the food of her ancestors. Which is particularly piquant, since she was adopted in China.

My mother-in-law's recipes, to me, to my child: That's the nature of inheritance. Nature, nurtured along to form individuals, each with a single identity.

CHAPTER FOUR

A Monk, Two Very Different Victorians, and the Knockout Mouse

How We Were Delivered the Genetics of Hair Color

IN 1865, the hunger moon rose on the eighth of February. Appearing deep in winter, the hunger moon is a marker, and contrary in its meaning: While it is full, the larders are not; if you have made it to then, your supplies are running low. The staples are wormy and your root vegetables are soft. Beneath its illumination, Gregor Mendel would take a cold walk, knowing only that he had done what he could. After cultivating peas for eight years, the monk was ready to present his work. Wanting to influence others to replicate his experiments, he gathered up a few plants and, lit by that moon, walked to the Realschule, the Austrian school where he taught physics and natural science, and where he would deliver a lecture sponsored by the Brünn Society for the Study of Natural Sciences.

Reading the paper took about an hour and, as the popular story goes, it was met with utter silence. Not a question from the audience of about forty; not a hand went up. Four weeks later Mendel read the second half of the paper. Again, there were no questions. The results of the research were unintelligible to all but a few scientists of the era and those few were not there.

It was during this second talk that the monk introduced what would later become known as Mendel's law. The first principle was that of segregation; the second, the law of independent assortment. Boiled down, Mendel's peas become the laws of inheritance, which dictate that specific factors are passed down from parents to offspring. These factors come in pairs, the offspring receiving one from each parent, one that will be dominant and the other recessive. But the traits do not blend: Tall and short does not make a medium-height pea or person; a black-haired and a white-haired parent do not result in gray-haired children. Nineteenth-century thought had almost universally assumed that they do. In genetics, it's one or the other. And what the Victorians made of red hair—a primary color, the others being yellow and blue, colors that even on an artist's palette you cannot achieve from the mixing of others—we pretty much know from literature: It was rare; it was odd; it was both feared and desired.

When the paper was published the following year, Mendel requested forty copies, which he sent to the people whose attention he desired. One of those was Charles Darwin. The manuscript was received at Darwin's great house in Downe and put on the library shelf, where it remained, uncut—the printed sheets folded into page-size segments but not split apart. Darwin, it seems, never read the paper Mendel sent him.

Nearly 140 years later, I looked for it on the shelves when

I went to Downe to visit. Had Darwin read Mendel's paper, it may have calmed him, reassured him that the discrete particles we inherit are more shuffled like a stack of recipe file index cards than they are blended into a flan. The paper may have eased any doubts Darwin had about his theory of natural selection, on how organisms evolve to fit their environment and how distinct changes in the inherited particles that aid in this fit have a better chance of survival than those that don't. These changes are called mutations, one of which had caused red hair in humans.

Traveling to Downe was part of what I came to think of as the genetic itinerary in the story of red hair, an attempt to understand the value of the single trait of red hair amid the enormity of the science of genetics. Wanting to establish the hair color's genetic status, I needed to know how the addition of science altered the identity of red hair as well as how the mutation that delivers red hair influences the survival of the wearer. Did the genetic change silently decide the redheads' fate by somehow making them rare, and, by association, target them for both the fear and desire I know exists?

The overt signs of red hair certainly had sealed the fate of its bearers in the unfortunate times of Set and the Inquisition and when it was needed as an ingredient for poison; they had marked redheads both in life and in the pages of the Bible, as well as those of literature. Hair color had suggested the redhead's purpose, meaning, message, and identity. Up until the discovery of genes, it would be fair to say that the color had defined the character of redheads. I wondered how the science of genetics had shaded those definitions of character, if at all.

Establishing the true identity of the redhead required the

same kind of inventory of the science of the hair color that had been made of the stories, myths, and rumors. Knowing that redheads thrive in the notoriously cloudy English climate made the trip to the British Isles essential; trying to understand the genetics, I brushed up on Mendel and then I went to Downe.

It's a lovely walk from the village to Darwin's house, the occasional car barely squeezing past on the lane cloistered in flora. It is peony season and the huge heads of pink, white, and magenta lay thugged by their own enthusiastic beauty, strewn along the path in my way.

Inside the house, the audiotape tour begins no less dramatically, in the drawing room, complete with piano, on which "the most dangerous man in Europe" laid out earthworms to sense if they could hear. This is the room where Charles Darwin played two games of backgammon every day and fell asleep as his wife read him novels. I love the idea that Darwin had his wife read him fiction and that he preferred stories with pretty heroines. This is the room, too, where, if the book he was reading was too big, he would split the spine into manageable hunks.

Sickly, wealthy, a curious amateur in a fine house, Darwin was freed by his conditions to think magnificent (some might say terrible) things. It is in his study where Darwin wrote up his pile of notes from five years spent sailing around the world on the *Beagle*, and in his study that he wrote and rewrote *On the Origin of Species*. The tiny cabinet drawers to the right of the mantel make it seem as though he never shook off his life at sea; they appear to be below-deck storage, small and unlikely to slide open in the tossing brine. The bookshelves are packed and, I am told, include the uncut manuscript by Mendel. Darwin disliked writing at a desk, instead spreading a writing board across the arms of the chair. This is a room of minute details, full of tweezers and picks, where eight years were spent classifying barnacles.

He took breaks to play billiards, in the next room. The Hopkins and Stephens table was paid for by selling his father's gold watch and other family heirlooms; a game or two was played every evening with Parslow, the butler. "I find it does me a deal of good & drives the horrid species out of my head," he wrote. Sometimes, though, he laid out species on the felt.

He broke from his work for a meal in the dining room every day at one o'clock, following his daily walk at noon. There are forty-eight settings of china in a botanical water lily theme. He and his wife had ten children, so there was much to do in here and yet the whole room orients outside—to a clematis limning the window and an ancient mulberry tree that was here when Darwin was alive. The garden can almost be touched from here, the very garden that gave him so much to consider. It is impossible to see the things he saw and not wonder what it was like to be fixed in this exact spot, knowing that it is your moment to ponder things that in their time are heretical or dangerous to consider, ideas that fly in the face of religion—to posit the scientific evolution of man.

Years ago a minister asked me, "Where is home?" I rattled off a few places; maybe it was my childhood town or college. Why?

"Home is the journey," he suggested.

Why, seven years after that conversation, am I walking around Darwin's house thinking that home is the journey? When done were the days of sailing on the *Beagle*, was home enough of a journey for Darwin? Now there are three voices in my head: a minister's, David Attenborough's (narrator of the audiotape), and my own. I flip off the cassette as I look out into the gardens, and something begins to goad me like a bee. For a sandlot thinker like me, this is about as close as I will ever get to thinking like Darwin: the voice of God, the sonorous voice of the upper-class Englishman, the voice of one's own fragile heart, all whorling in my head at once.

Darwin not only had the religion of the Victorians—in fact his wife, Emma, was devout and feared for her husband in the afterlife—but he also served as the tipping point for so many believers, who upon meeting his science slid into disbelief. Alongside that was his Edinburgh and Cambridge education, and then his own intuitive heart.

Intuition tells me that there is more at work as I peer at the garden than I am willing to accept, that something deeply personal is shifting. Wondering just what is, I wander into what may have been a bedroom and where now are bug boxes and fish, specimens Darwin observed, things he learned to skin and stuff at the University of Edinburgh. Suddenly in view are two dozen hummingbirds under a huge domed cloche, the top bird so bright red that the color defies reasonable explanation. And then, just as fast, the shade is mere background to a competing vibrancy—a color so quiveringly orange on the head of a little girl, staring eye-to-eye at me through the glass.

Both of us are bending over and, in tempo, we both straighten, smiling hugely at one another.

"Hello." Hers is an English country accent. She is nine, I suspect, maybe in third grade.

"Hi."

She looks so familiar that I look away to focus my thoughts. We are surrounded by puffer fish and freckled porcupine fish, cactus finch, warbler finch, and all manner of collected creatures, on cotton, stuffed mounted, and tagged. The room is alive with dead specimens, ringed with posters of varying heights explaining hunks of Darwin's thinking. He started a series of notebooks shortly after returning from the voyage and within a few months was convinced that all creatures were gradually and constantly changing, that evolution was taking place. Labeling the idea "transmutation of species," he realized that every living organism was part of a tree of life with many branches. But he still didn't know how evolution happened. Reading Malthus, Darwin posited that those who survived and reproduced were most suited or adapted to their way of life, a kind of natural selection; he concluded that some characteristics that helped the individual to survive in the first place are passed along and that over time these small differences add up to larger, more noticeable ones.

And then there she is, the little girl with red hair—an example of Darwin's theory of change, a living human specimen of something that survived and was passed on to become a noticeable change, a mutation of color. There she stands, on the landmass where the greatest numbers of redheads in the world thrive; here in the home of the man who described the origin of us all. She is a mutation, and so am I.

Mutations spice things up. Random genetic accidents that change the order of the AGTC's in our DNA, they change the genome of an organism. They greatly increase genetic diversity. Change a letter in a word in English and *rid* becomes *red*. Change a letter in the DNA and you might change humanity. Except that natural selection is exquisitely efficient at eliminating mutations that affect important functional parts of the genome—the genes, for example—leaving all humans pretty much the same. In fact, genetically, at least, humans are 99.9 percent alike, with only about one in every thousand human base pairs varying among individuals. That we look different, therefore, may be genetically insignificant despite the fact that we make so much of our different appearances.

Seeing that red-haired child and how much we were alike—the hair color, the freckled nose, the pale skin—tweaked that same private place that was provoked at witch camp, reminding me that a simple pursuit can turn personal in a flash. By following this genetic itinerary, I was not idly drifting in the wake of this gene, as I had thought, not merely following up a lead by doing some reporting. I was pursuing myself, wondering how much, if at all, exploring the genetics of a hair color might alter my own sense of identity. I realized that in the same way the gene had moved through the world and onto that child's red head, it had done so through the myriad people in history who mated and moved the gene along to me. I started to count up red-haired relatives.

On both my parents' sides, the family could be traced back to England. On my mother's side it was possible to name names right up to passengers disembarking from a ship in New England in the 1600s and to run a bloodline through the scrappy New England patriot Ethan Allen, leader of the first victory in the American Revolution. His midnight taking of Fort Ticonderoga was endlessly reenacted in my tomboy childhood. "By what authority?" demands the awakened British officer (the part that was always hard to get some kid to play, but I had to find someone, so I could then shout, "In the name of the Great Jehovah and the Continental Congress!"). Though no portraits of Ethan Allen survive, it is known that he was a hard-drinking, bombastic personality who towered over most men at six foot four with his unkempt mane of red hair. His lineage is well documented, with the genes of our common revolutionary drifting from New England to about as far north in New York as one can go, where my relatives settled along the St. Lawrence River in Massena, eventually moving to Wisconsin and then back to New York with my grandfather Harold Allen Zillmann. His genes flowed into his only child, my mother, Allene, a brunette, named for the famous revolutionary redhead.

On my father's side I knew that some of my English relatives had red hair, all pretty much like mine, which is now the color of varnish on teak. Not orange. Not brown. Not curly, but not utterly straight; were it water, it would have a current, this underneath life that waves just enough to keep the top in motion. My father, his mother, and I had this same shade: brighter in youth, darkening with age. The three of us also have freckles, long legs, high brows, and hazel eyes, the combination making us look very much alike over three generations.

My parents, both newspaper reporters, met in the press box at Belmont Park, a New York racetrack. During the Saratoga meet in 1953, their genes recombined to produce my brown-haired, blue-eyed sister, whose middle name is High Gun, borrowed from the 1954 Belmont Stakes winner. Blessedly conceived after any of the three stakes races of the Triple Crown and before those run in the year I was born, I was left with only a first and last name. Apparently, we are a sporting breed, though when ranking what I received from my parents, that's not what I think of first, always rating my red hair as my best inheritance. And yet I could only name two people from whom I'd received it.

Before I left for the United Kingdom I had hired a British genealogist to track down anything he could, knowing that official documents—army papers, merchant seaman registrations, church records—frequently record the hair color of individuals. Besides those of my English grandparents, I had only two names—but no physical description for either person—written in my grandfather's uneven hand:

"My mother's name was Annie Madsen Johnston. Her father drowned in the River Mersey when she was ten. Alexander Johnston. 1865. He was a Dane. A ship's rigger."

When viewed through the lens of red hair, my grandfather's scrawl about the Danish rigger took on some interest and I wondered if the drowned man had been a redhead. My grandfather was not red-haired but his son, my father, was. So someone further back in that line must have been, as well. I knew that while the idea that all Danes have Viking blood and that all Vikings are red-haired was a gross misunderstanding of many things, at the core was the truth that purely in terms of hair color, a Dane, originating from an area of fair-haired, fair-skinned people, had an increased chance of being a redhead. But the British genealogist turned over little except to report that a drowning in the swift Mersey would produce no body, that no body meant no death certificate—coroner's rules. The genealogist did provide a marriage certificate of the rigger's daughter, my English grandfather's mother, confirming the rigger's name, occupation, and deceased status at the time of the nuptials.

In other families, there might be a family Bible with names and dates of birth and death. Not in mine. During the Victorian era my English family had abandoned their belief in God. My father told me, as it was told to him, that they were not alone. By 1865, confronted by the great recent scientific discoveries, Victorians en masse experienced a tremendous loss of faith. The cotton gin had been around for nearly one hundred years and the Industrial Revolution was terrible in its wonder: powerful in what it could do, frightening in what it made obsolete. After Darwin published *On the Origin of Species* in 1859, many great writers and intellectuals—and soon, people like my family—wrestled with their faith, wondering if God himself was to be removed from the workings of their daily lives. We might think that the dislodging of faith would turn people's faces toward the cool hand of science for comfort and reassurance about their origins, as well as their equality with one another. It didn't. In hindsight, it appears that when with one hand Charles Darwin provided us with the science to understand our common humanity, with the other he handed us a whip with which to flail anyone who looked unlike ourselves.

I knew my English grandfather, my father's father, John Lewis Roach. Born in 1881, he lived under Victoria's reign. A light heavyweight boxer from Liverpool, he was, as well, a carpenter, chauffeur, professional horseplayer, and occasional breeder of Chow Chows. He lived with us and was the family cook. Though I loved him, it's fair to say that he didn't like anyone but family, having a racist appellation for everyone else. Among those he disliked were the Scottish, Italians, Germans, Welsh, Dutch, Indians, anyone Asian, everyone African, as well as Londoners. But his greatest venom was reserved for the Irish, who, fleeing the poverty of their own land, had been hurled in huge numbers into his English hometown on the Irish Sea. He had a great deal to say about them, none of which I shall repeat, except to say that whenever anyone I meet reveals that languid aspiration to speak like, dress like, or live in a house built by a Victorian, I'm sure they don't mean him. They mean the Darwin kind. They surely don't mean my type of Victorian, the ones drawn by Dickens.

It was my English grandfather who taught me about the prescriptions against seeing redheads on the dock or aboard ship; the one who stood in the doorway at midnight on New Year's Eve. And in the years approaching his hundredth birthday, he bequeathed to me his curious pile of possessions: an ivory mah-jongg set, a silver flask decorated with a Japanese garden, and a glass slide harboring a shadowy silver image jammed inextricably into a cheap metal frame. Taken as they are, they remind me of Wemmick, Mr. Jagger's clerk in Dickens's *Great Expectations*. Wemmick warns Pip to always get the "portable property." These were portable all right. They were all my grandfather had. He brought little more than that to his new world. Believing he was leaving behind the poverty that he blamed on the Irish, and hating them as he did, he came to America at the turn of the century, only to discover that when his fianceé followed him in 1906, marrying him the day after her arrival, their neighbors in Brooklyn thought his wife was Irish, basing this identity, he always said, on a single trait: the color of her hair.

Contrary to popular notion, it was Herbert Spencer, an English philosopher and contemporary of Darwin, who coined the term "survival of the fittest." Also from Spencer's work comes the term "social Darwinism," though in the misunderstanding born of time and distance, both phrases are wrongly attributed to Darwin. For a while, social Darwinism tidily explained why people with advantages beget children with the same advantages, deeming those advantageous far fitter than others and by extension, more suited to survive. But this theory worked to explain the rungs of society only until those who had it all began to be outnumbered by those who had nothing.

During the middle to late 1800s, more than three million Irish immigrants entered the United States, predominantly because of the deplorable conditions in their country during and after the potato famine. Before and just after World War I the immigration of eastern and southern Europeans spiked. The result was that in the first fifteen years of the 1900s, immigration was responsible for half of the population growth in the United States. Soon, despite the country's preferred reputation as a melting pot, not everyone was pleased by the ingredients now in the stew.

It was in this climate that the new science of genetics was used by some to identify which of the world's people might become a burden to society. Because society was, indeed, burdened. By the end of the nineteenth century, workhouses in England were full to overflowing; the slums of New York City were teeming. Entering the new century, the upper-class "them" in both America and England were engaged in discussion as to how to deal with the underclass "us." And while the bulk of the kinder form of concern was about the feeble-minded and those who could not care for themselves, the argument soon extended to anyone who might be less desirable to have around. How to identify these people was the key.

One method was by applying social Darwinism to eugenics. The term *eugenics* was coined by Francis Galton, a cousin and contemporary of Darwin. At its worst, it was Hitler's hateful science in which the fittest race was granted biological sanctity and bestowed a superior status. But Hitler did not formulate the ideals he embraced. He and his scientists adopted these ideas as part of a huge movement of social Darwinist eugenics that burned through the first thirty years of the twentieth century. The German version was adopted from the American model.

During my course of research, several people had suggested that Hitler had banned the marriage of two redheads, fearing their offspring would be "deviant." Much like the "all redheads are witches" notion, it seemed not to have ever been so stated or enacted in the form of legislation. Yet I wondered if, as with the witches and the surprising menstrual blood connection, in tracing the Hitler rumor to its source, I might discover something illuminating along the way.

The American eugenics movement was begun in 1904, with a grant from the Carnegie Institute of Washington, when a station was set up in Cold Spring Harbor, New York, to study experimental evolution. Headed by Charles Davenport, the lab worked with poultry and canaries and made significant contributions to the study of Mendelian inheritance. But when they cast their light on humans, they did so through the lens of eugenics, the science of improving the human race by giving the more "suitable" races a better, faster chance of predominating.

Francis Galton was often heard to say, "Whenever you can, count." His particular mix of looking and counting spawned the mathematics of heredity, which in turn established a relationship between the existence of our hereditary traits and our ability to measure them. Looking and counting was what the eugenicists did first, studying humans by dividing them by the observable Mendelian traits of hair color, eye color, hair texture, and pigment.

Records of the American Eugenics Records Office are kept by the American Philosophical Society, housed in Philosophic Hall, a prim brick building anchoring the west side of Philadelphia's Independence Square. The oldest surviving learned organization in the country, the society was founded in 1743 by Benjamin Franklin. The society's sparsely occupied library has an assured Ralph Lauren décor. The paint is a putty shade and the wood tables, complete with green-glass-shaded reading lamps, are highly polished over their clean lines. The people who read there turn pages quietly or type onto laptops with the most deferential of touch. Busts and portraits of Franklin look down on this bastion of substantial quiet, encouraging the most patient behavior; I actually clasped my hands at my table while waiting for someone to bring me the files on hair and hair color from the Eugenics Records Office.

Opening the files for the first time, flipping through the manila tabs denoting their contents, I quickly notice that the boxes look like recipe files. I dismiss the image as not sober enough, get up, stretch, admire a couple of busts and a portrait or two of Benjamin Franklin, then sit back down and start again, only to have the image return as I scan the protruding tabs on which were written: Fingerprints. Hair. Hair Color. It looks like a recipe for the nature of man, listed one ingredient at a time. But I'm not quite right in this, because the eugenicists' idea was not to include all these ingredients but to identify which to leave out—say, a hair

color that carried with it a trait of lesser human nature—
with the goal of nurturing a fitter mankind.

American eugenicists hoped to control the flow of immigrants by reducing the number and raising the qualifica-
tions for entry. Those who were already citizens were
encouraged to write in to the eugenics lab, describe their
ethnic backgrounds, and let it be determined whether their
future progeny would create a "fitter family." If not, it was
hoped that those people could be discouraged from marrying. To assist in their plans, the American eugenicists
collected pedigree data in the very files that look to me
like recipes.

The human beings immortalized in the files within the
box specifically on red hair all have many other qualities, of
course, but they have been sorted and filed by this single
trait. Here are pages of testimony taken from red-haired
people about how they came by this one trait: "My father
had red hair. So do I." Or, "My father and his father had
red hair, I do not." This accumulated data makes sense in
light of Davenport's initial research, which was in Mendelian inheritance of eye color, hair color, hair texture, and
pigmentation. Where the eugenicists went wrong was in
their strategy to prevent conditions such as pauperism,
relying upon their assumption that not only did shiftlessness
lead to pauperism but also that traits such as shiftlessness
were inherited.

The eugenicists were dogged in their task of acquiring
information. Questionnaires include single-trait sheets, beginning with a brief personal description, and individual
analysis cards, inquiring about physical traits, illnesses, hair
type, gait, speech, handedness. They include a section titled
Mental, where interviewees rate themselves in memory,

imagination, predilection to art, craftsmanship, letters, social service, and business. Questions dealing with temperament request that the subject underscore traits to identify themselves within categories including "narrowness in views," "interest in world events," "reactions to adversity," and "reaction to success," which may include "elation," "conceit," or "rests on oars." Some attached pictures of themselves. Sorting through the files, it is possible to see how one might erroneously conclude, for instance, that redheads who rest on their oars also spend lots of money, are fretful, and occasionally walk in their sleep.

Eventually the American eugenicists were responsible for what today seem to be remarkable policy decisions. Not only did the federal government restrict the immigration of those deemed less fit, but according to the archival records of the American Philosophical Society, at one time or another, thirty-three American states also enacted statutes under which the involuntary sterilization of more than sixty thousand Americans was performed. Sterilization of people in institutions continued into the mid-1970s.

Those facts are well documented. What is also understood is that the American version of eugenics influenced Hitler's scientists, as documented in books such as Daniel Kevles's *In the Name of Eugenics*, as well as in the published material of the American Philosophical Society. And while nowhere in these files is it stated that redheads are deviant and should be banned from marrying one another, the documents do reveal associations along physiognomic lines linking pigment to temperament and suggesting that some of these lines be excluded from the full privileges of citizenship. Exported to Germany under the Third Reich, these ideas of exclusion suggest frightening links to the historic association between red hair and the Jews.

Unlike their European cousin, American eugenics studies were not used to separate Anglo from Gypsy or even white from black but rather to distance the blood of the "original" settlers of America—the Puritans of Anglo stock—from other whites, specifically the Catholics and the Jews. When judging these other, "lesser" whites, the American eugenicists relied on rankings of scholastic intelligence, which appeared to rate these immigrants far below America's tenured citizens. This, coupled with higher birth rates among the poor, fed the fear that resulted in an association between a weak intellect and a high sex drive, the latter of which, by that time, was already strongly associated with red-haired women.

Sex was a hot topic in both the American and British versions of eugenics. The bulging underclasses were out-reproducing the upper classes, and, it was assumed, overwhelming not only the physical traits of their superiors but also their privileged way of life. The masses were seen as stampeding in numbers toward imposing upon all of society the immorality believed to come from living in the filth and the depravity that traveled with a lack of education. Nothing scared the upper classes like the impending parity of the masses. There was a desperate feeling that something was shifting, that the good stock was being diluted. While not in the same league as the fear and hatred of the Jews, Gypsies, and homosexuals, the discrimination of the Irish—perhaps a mere middling form of hatred—was acutely felt by those immigrants.

To the English Victorian, the Irish were an overbreeding, simpleminded, story telling, childlike people who needed protection and who practiced an absurd religion full of accessories only a child would require to hold his interest—the garish accoutrements of the Catholic Church: its confession, its idolatry exhibited in its crucifixes, and its rosary beads. Practical and irreligious, my English Victorian grandfather was no exception in his disdain for such accessorized worship. In what he chose to carry with him to his new life, there is no Bible, no cross, nor any article of faith. Instead, he emigrated with little more than a flask, a single glass slide of a man sitting in a chair, and a mah-jongg set.

Seen in the light of the tale of red hair, his curation in these scant inheritances braids me deeper into the story. In two ways, these objects provide me with a physical link to the times in which he lived. First, the items represent a Victorian obsession, literally a mania that ensued following the opening of the East to the West. After a series of treaties granted access, English and American Victorians clamored to get their hands on all things Asian. Tea was imported in great quantities; lacquer and porcelain began to brighten the dark woods of the Victorian home; smaller objects—a flask, a game— found their ways into lesser households. Simultaneously, there was the new medium of photography, which Charles Dickens had said was among the three things that were "clamorously required of Man in the miscellaneous thoroughfares of the metropolis": that he have his boots cleaned, eat a penny ice, and, "thirdly, that he get himself photographed." Clearly someone who meant a great deal to my grandfather had done just that, as evidenced by the presence of the single glass slide.

In their other role, my grandfather's items illustrate how things can change identity when pressed into a new kind of service. Much like an object of fear during a time of belief in sympathetic magic becomes an object of desire when an age of reason dawns, or an ancient, terrifying female demon becomes a symbol of modern woman's sexual freedom, my grandfather's possessions change roles when moving from his English Victorian hands to my American twenty-first-century scrutiny. Doing so, they parallel another aspect of this tale, told by perhaps the most important of all Victorian curios, arguably the generation's smallest collectible that when changing hands, changed jobs. A little, live ball of fur, it became the delivery mechanism for nothing less than the proof of the work of Darwin and Mendel, attesting to nothing less than the existence of the science of genetics. It is the mouse.

The mouse was in good company, there among tea, porcelains, and lacquered furniture, all three of which passed into acquisitive English and American hands as fast as ships could unload them. Not that we didn't have our own mice. Around the time dinosaurs were disappearing and mammals emerging—about seventy-five million years ago—the mouse and man split off from a common ancestor. Both inherited upwards of twenty thousand genes from that shared kin, forever linking mouse and man through common ingredients of their separate identities.

The first written reference to nonwild mice was in China in 1100 B.C.E. Evidence suggests that in China and Japan there existed an early fondness for selecting mice with unusual coat colors and experimenting with their breeding. By C.E. 300, mouse breeding was a popular pastime in China; the animals came in spotted, black-eyed white, albino, yellow, dove, and waltzing (a mouse with a specific genetic mutation that made it walk in circles). In 1787, *The Breeding of Curious Varieties of the Mouse* was published in Kyoto. It included drawings as well as recipes for creating specific colors. After the 1854 treaty of Kanagawa opened the ports, European visitors, enchanted with the hobby, brought it home, never suspecting that embedded in that import was the study of how genes behave. Once a mere parlor pastime, this sea change in the lives of mice began with the publication of Darwin's *On the Origin of Species* in 1859 and after Mendel raised more than 28,000 pea plants, analyzed them, established the laws of heredity, coined the genetics terms *dominance* and *recessiveness*, published his work, and died with little attention.

In the 1870s, Englishman Walter Maxey got his first mouse. The breadth of his adoration for the tiny creature would eventually garner him the moniker "Father of the Mouse Fancy." He established the National Mouse Club of England in 1895 which, in turn, set breeding standards and produced the first mouse show. Soon it seemed that everyone had to have a mouse—a little living thing that, when bred with another mouse, resulted in the most astonishing fun with color, living color. The infatuation with the fancy mice traveled to Americans from their English Victorian friends.

In 1900, Mendel made his comeback, posthumously, when three independent papers "rediscovered" the rules of inheritance, rescued the monk from oblivion, and launched the science soon to be known as genetics. But Mendel's works were based on plants. And, simultaneously, Galton's very popular work was pushing the theory that traits blended together, any one of those traits potentially contaminating a whole population.

Suddenly, there was something to disprove, something to test and something to test it on. And mice, who travel well and breed regularly, make a much better genetic study than, say, peas. Or humans, for that matter, who are both slow to replicate and who, as exhibited by Galton and the eugenicists, carry to the study of one another's pigment far too much cultural baggage. In the mouse, the theories of Mendel and Darwin could be seen in the colors of the coats produced from crossbreeding. At first figuring that crossing a black and a white mouse would produce a gray one, the scientists found they were wrong and became more curious.

By the beginning of the twentieth century, scientists were testing patterns of inheritance by breeding different fancy mice. In the process, they produced some of the forerunners of the modern lab mouse, including the agouti, whose black or brown fur contains yellow areas on each hair. Mutant forms of the agouti gene can cause the animals to have yellow coats as well as several known medical conditions, including obesity.

A few years into the new century, a French geneticist studying the agouti mouse found that when the yellow variety mate, the result is always two yellows for every normal agouti. He concluded that yellow is a dominant version, or allele, for the agouti gene. This didn't jive with the laws Mendel laid out, however, which held that the union would result in three yellow for every one agouti. Soon, work in the Harvard lab led by William Ernest Castle revealed that the missing mouse had in fact died in utero because having two copies of the yellow gene is lethal. And so, along with patterns of color, the very first deadly allele was revealed, and with it the first of the many pathways the pigmentary system provides in human development and disease.

There are two types of pigment in hair and skin: eumelanin, which is brown or black, and phaeomelanin, which is red or yellow. Years of studying mouse coat colors allowed researchers to make many observations about the inheritance of pigment but few about what pigment is for. That would have to wait for the scientific understanding that could only come with the study of bacteria and viruses, which, in turn, allowed for the identification of genes at the molecular level.

To make progress in the world of genetic laboratory research, you need a knockout mouse. It is a moniker particularly appealing in the study of redheads. To be a knockout in this case, however, the mouse must resemble the human phenotype you want to research—in this case red hair, which, in mice, appears as the yellow variety of phaeomelanin. After identifying that gene leading to the hair color, you must then knock it out by breeding a mouse missing that gene, or knock out another quality and see what travels with it. It is the primary way of studying the function of genes: rendering dysfunctional the desired gene and observing what happens to the animal. For instance, to study obesity, you would knock out a gene and if the mouse became overweight without it, you would assume that the gene somehow is involved in the regulation of body weight, appetite, or fat cell creation.

And, in doing that, you might discover that the recessive allele for red hair is linked to the body's ability to store fat. This is what Oregon endocrinologist Roger Cone was researching in the early 1990s when he noticed, among other things, that his mutant mice with yellow hair produced relatively more phaeomelanin than eumelanin. (It was not all work and no play at the lab; some members formed a softball team named the Lethal Yellows, for the deadly version that results from having two yellow alleles.)

Cone went on to clone the gene underlying the presence of yellow hair in mice—the melanocortin I receptor, or MC1R—and showed that some of the mutations involved meant that MC1R did not work, as a result of the gene's protein losing some or all of its abilities. In genetics this is called a loss of function mutation. Mice in which both copies of the gene were nonfunctional produce excess phaeomelanin compared to eumelanin and the result is yellow fur—which would be red in humans.

Cone had discovered the gene for red hair—in mice—and in his original paper he included the tantalizing suggestion that it might also play an important role in human pigmentation. And reading that, half a world away, was Jonathan Rees, a scientist living in a city of redheads. And it got him thinking.

Digestif

Recipe for a Heritage

B AKING IS NOT supposed to bring out the worst in anyone.

And yet, my friend Phoebe tells a story of a cook she knew growing up whose dominant trait was leaving out a key ingredient when passing along her recipes. Oh, the woman was a marvel: a covered dish for every potluck supper, funeral casseroles, wedding brunch quiche. She rose to every occasion, as did her soufflés.

But not when she passed along the recipes. Right by the kitchen phone when the recipient called, she'd commiserate over the flat frittata, the dry chocolate cake, the sweet lemon squares. Leaving out the ingredient meant that hers could never be replicated. Hers were not to be cloned.

She is what we might call a carrier: While she's got the goods, she's not giving them up. In genetics, she's a heterozygote: Got 'em, but possibly keeping them to herself. The counterpart to the carrier is known in genetics as the affected, the homozygote. Having two genetic changes for the same thing—two alleles for the changes that result in red hair, for instance—homozygotes are givers, passing along their trait without hesitation. They can't help themselves.

What the recipient does with those ingredients varies. Everyone has two copies of every gene, one from our mother and one from our father. If you have both genetic changes that lead to red hair, then you will have red hair. However, if you only have one change, you have an increased chance but no certainty of having the color; you have some of the genetic material but perhaps nothing to show for it. This is called an autosomal mode of inheritance and in practice means that while both parents may not have red hair, they could, in fact, both be carriers of the red-hair gene. In this case, perhaps one in four of their children might have red hair.

Among the types of red hair—everything along the spectrum, from strawberry blond to dark auburn—the genetics are fairly similar. However, bright-red-haired people are much more likely to carry two different copies of the gene than, say, strawberry blonds. If one parent has bright red hair, therefore carrying two copies of the gene (one on each of the chromosomes), and the other parent is a carrier, perhaps half of their children would have red hair, as in my family. This also explains why the hair color might skip a generation, though it's a popular misconception that it *always* does.

A heritage is something that comes to us or belongs to us by reason of birth. It does not skip along, though it can be altered. Part of my heritage is my hair color as well as how it is perceived, both of which were passed along from others. To travel into me, the gene for red hair had to hurtle through thousands of years of individuals before it funneled down into the people I can name. I had no say in my genetic inheritance and, similarly, via the birthright, no say in how my hair color may be perceived by the casual observer. How I respond is what I can change.

Looking up and down a redheaded woman, running your eyes over her, what do you see? What you are taught to see, given the time and place you are taught to see it. That's part of your heritage and through it, you may make your own observations, on your own terms, by knocking out some associations and adding others.

How does the redhead feel about being looked at? Reflecting her own heritage, her responses will differ depending on who is doing the looking.

One particular redhead comes into focus when measuring how my own heritage has been viewed. From her experiences, I inherited some of my own responses about being regarded.

So look at her. Standing alone in a crowd, Margaret Pilkington was tall, tugging along a domed wooden case, shellacked almost the same color as her red hair. Go with what you've got. It was an adage, even then, six years into the new century, in northwest England, on the Mersey River, as the heavy SS *Teutonic* barely bobbed, quietly awaiting its next load off to America. Freckled, with long legs, a broad forehead, and large, strong hands, she was dressed in white simplicity, dragging with her everything she would take into her new life. Carrying the genes that made her look Irish. Indeed, she could not have looked more Irish, unless she opened her mouth, at which point she could not have sounded more English.

But, as Henry Higgins would later sing in *My Fair Lady*, "An Englishman's way of speaking absolutely classifies him; the moment he talks he makes some other Englishman despise him." (George Bernard Shaw, a eugenics supporter, wrote *Pygmalion*, the play on which the musical is based.) And though she was English, she had her own sound; not that southern English dialect we now think of as BBC English, nor the King's, but a dialect called Scouse, from northern England, specifically from Liverpool. It emigrated during the Irish potato famine, which heaved a tremendous wave of desperate people from Ireland straight across the sea to Liverpool and, with them, came the very timbre of their talk. The languages sifted together to form this unique sound, more Beatles than Tudors, more us than them.

If the "them" were watching, they couldn't know that she would never come back. They could only hope that she would never see English soil again, but they couldn't know that one world war, the birth of her redheaded son, and then the advent of the next world war would prevent her from ever going home. And so she took what she could carry and walked up to the Mersey's edge, where she may have paused, knowing the story of the drowning of the rigger, her fiancé's grandfather. But she did not pray, nodding instead to the water in recognition of her own survival, the only faith left to her, mistaken in her belief that she was leaving all this senseless hatred behind.

A "them" of the world would have watched her leave with good riddance. Another one of those people, over-running the population with their sickly traits, plain as day, plain as the hair on her head, don't you know, look at that, let her leave.

And isn't it all in the eye of the beholder, God's great joke that we can't see ourselves and what we look like as we cringe, laugh, or cry, or as we leave the land we love behind?

But in another of God's great jokes, one man's red wig is another man's desire; what makes someone's blood boil engorges another with something else entirely. My English grandfather would tell me, years after she died, that what he loved most about my grandmother, Margaret Pilkington Roach, was what he did every single night of his marriage until the very day she died: To sit on the end of their marital bed—first in Brooklyn, then in the Rockaways, then out in Great Neck, and later in Manhattan—and watch her plait her long red hair. Had she not, they would both have tangled in it in the night. And so they sat and talked while first she brushed then combed and then braided her hair into two long red plaits. And then they would climb into bed.

CHAPTER FIVE

The Itch of Genetics/
The Genetics of Itch

*Science Has Done Little
to Extinguish the Fire of the Tale*

B Y T H E T I M E I get to Oxford, I am expecting a good
show: computers and lasers, maybe, certainly over-
heads, test tubes, vector charts, the whole shebang. And
so it is with real disappointment that I watch while Professor Rosalind Harding searches madly for a pencil and a
piece of paper in her little office. I had read about Harding a
few months before arriving here, when, according to press
accounts, she had dated the gene for red hair and an-
nounced that redheads are Neanderthals.

It seemed unlikely. Neanderthals are easy to picture. They
have been cartooned so many times—the heavy brow
looming over a short, squat torso—having fascinated us
since the first of their fossils were found in 1856 and having
been subject to wild conjecture and mystery. Neanderthals,
we now know, were one of perhaps four contemporaneous
prehistoric peoples on Earth, who lived mostly in Europe

and parts of Asia and vanished about 33,000 years ago. For many, they are humanoid dinosaurs and hold a similar mystique, especially when you consider that they are their own species.

Upright, similar to modern humans, they have taken a lot of bashing over the years. We forget that they managed to survive in the harshest conditions for longer than modern man has in much gentler times. So we slander them, calling our boyfriends Neanderthal. They fascinate me for several reasons, not the least of which is that they sprinkled the bodies of their dead in red pigments, apparently to resuscitate the deceased's color back to the warm tones of life and blood.

But Rosalind Harding, a population geneticist at the hallowed halls of Oxford, never said that redheads are Neanderthals, though I had read that she had pretty much everywhere. I admit, it is that misquote that made me pick up the phone and call her, and when I did, she made it exactingly clear, in her crisp Australian cadence, that if I was calling about that and I was going to come all the way to Oxford to see her, I shouldn't bother because that was not at all what she had said. Fine.

On the plane over, I reread the newspaper pieces, my favorite being the one from 2000 in the Scottish press claiming that Scots, being redheads by nature, were therefore directly descended from Neanderthals and that those genetics finally explain their "fearsome reputation for causing trouble." If only it were that simple.

Standing in her office as she looked for a pencil, I ask, "So how about that Neanderthal thing?" First question.

Rosalind Harding is a compact woman whose precision extends to the laugh lines that instantly gather her face. She is "comfortable" with the "elegance" of mathematics, she tells me, as a way of introducing the splicing of math and genetics required for her particular way of studying human origins. She looks like she loves math: Her rumpled T-shirt takes a defiant stand for chaos theory, clashing with the dreamy images of robed students wafting over the rainy lanes of Oxford. And she sounds like she keeps a proper perspective on her subjects. Her use of the word "humans" distances them somehow, putting them at the other end of a zoom lens, those two-legged creatures scrambling around in a petri dish.

Population genetics involves studying the genetic structures of populations and how they change over time. The science is rigorous but depends on certain genetic and statistic principles that give it both appeal and pitfalls. And because it is science, there is no Bible—or bible, for that matter. There are methods of interpretation, there are some historic facts, and there are assumptions.

Some members of the press assumed that since the gene for red hair emerged while Neanderthals were roaming the planet, the hair color showed up in that species. They were wrong, but the misunderstanding makes a good illustration of how we tell biological time, specifically how we date when humans diverged from the rest of the natural world.

The date of divergence of one population from another is proved by measuring how long those two populations have been separate as well as just how biologically separate they have become over time. To do so, scientists use what is commonly called a "molecular clock," which, for example, dates human separation from chimpanzees at roughly five million years ago.

Through this method it was proved that no trace of

Neanderthal DNA entered our gene pool and that we are genetically distinct from that other species, but that Neanderthals have more in common with sequenced human DNA than they do with sequenced chimpanzee DNA. In other words, while the molecular clock allows us to see our differences, it also forces us to recognize how remarkably close we are.

Rosalind Harding's science lives right here on the cusp, measuring one while recognizing the other: She is looking at our diversity—when, for instance red hair emerged on humans—all the while depending on the clock that ticks off our commonalities. And for that, she uses a pencil.

The formula used for the mathematical basis of population genetics predicts the expected genotype frequencies based on allele frequencies. If the observed frequencies do not show a significant deviation from those that were expected, the population is said to be in Hardy-Weinberg equilibrium (HWE, named for Godfrey Harold Hardy, a British mathematician, and Wilhelm Weinberg, a German physician, the authors of the law) and certain assumptions about the population can be made. Any change from HWE and certain other assumptions are made.

Assumptions rile science. When comparing only two of the schools of thought within the study of human origin, basic differences arise: The statistics of population genetics may not always match dates with actual events, for instance; physical anthropologists, who study human origins from fossils and artifacts, benefit from radiocarbon analysis and, as a result, believe their data to be more firm than that of population genetics. It is possible that we will never fully agree on who lived where and when. But it is also possible that much of the tale of human migration and drift can be seen in the colors of our hair and skin, that these very differences that have caused such historical and social separations also carry in them important information about our evolution.

No wonder the press piped the Neanderthal quote; it's a bite, though an inaccurate one, of a meaty issue. Trying to match the emergence of the gene to a confirmed simultaneous event in history, a reporter had asked Harding if the gene coincided with the Neanderthal era, to which she had to concede that it did, roughly. And so the idea that the gene appeared on the heads of Neanderthals was mistakenly born.

Offered as a small example of a huge disagreement between the sciences, and the difficulty of lay readers to accurately understand research, the misunderstanding about the Neanderthal doesn't even begin to address the differences within the statistics field itself. These include the simple fact that within the mathematically based field of dating genetic frequency, there are those who rely on newly available software and those what don't.

Looking at Harding scribble, watching her work, I am reminded of all the times I've found myself face-to-face with someone in pursuit. Whether on the faces of scientists, detectives, or anyone else chasing the truth, I have seen this look before and it leads me to believe that the real top note of desire is pursuit. The conquest—desire's reward—is what satisfies us, but pursuit thrills us.

What Harding looks like is called her phenotype: what traits an organism has—how she appears and, to some extent, how she behaves. What underlies that is her genotype, what genes an organism carries and how the alleles, the contrasting genes for the same trait (tall, short), behave. Harding's genotype makes her small, brown-haired, and probably contributes to her being smart enough to get where she is. And since the gene for language has been mapped, we know how she does what she does for a living and why.

The genotype expresses itself to some degree in the phenotype, although the genotype also carries the imprint of those things we inherit but that are not expressed. The genotype carries all of our alleles, those contrasting genes for the same trait. Each trait is determined by one or a few genes. And there are somewhere in the neighborhood of 25,000 genes in the human body. This is where things explode: To study the genetic structure of a whole population, you would have to look at the total number of all alleles in everyone. Population geneticists calculate the frequency of alleles, tracking whether alleles disappear or become more frequent over time. Which is why when you read about population genetics in the popular press, it is likely to be either in some absurd quote about Neanderthals or in a complex examination of some huge evolutionary debate that is balancing on the head of a genetic pin.

A few years ago headlines around the world trumpeted that the ancestors of Africans and non-Africans split apart nearly 200,000 years ago, much earlier than had previously been believed. And six or so paragraphs into every article, it was revealed that the entire study and resulting monumental claim rested on one small gene. Later in the piece would come the requisite quote from the lead researcher about how they chose that gene because it was convenient.

In this, Harding is no exception: She is utterly nonplused by my phenotype—"Doesn't interest me a bit," she says, glancing up, perhaps noticing for the first time that I am, in fact, a redhead. But the gene, she likes.

"Because it is a tidy package," she offers. "Small" is how she describes the mutation for red hair, making the study of it more "elegant" when figuring the expected genotype frequencies using allele frequencies going back those five million years since man split from the apes. The mutation's economy makes it easier to find the redhead in the haystack of hair color. And what Harding found is that the gene emerged somewhere around fifty thousand years ago.

I remember hair color and skin color being the popular examples used in high school biology, quoted as practical examples of genetics. Everyone got the dominant-recessive lesson using the example of red hair and blue eyes, so we all grew up believing that you have two copies of every gene, one from your father and one from your mother, and that both had to be genes for red hair in order for you to be a redhead. Red hair was rare and even when it occurred in a family, we were instructed, it always skipped a generation. This last concept made me raise my hand in Mrs. Smith's eighth grade biology class to report that not only I, but my father and his mother too, all had red hair, but that my mother did not, a contribution that got me scolded for being the troublemaker that I was.

Some of what we learned in biology was correct, of course. We do get two copies; red hair is a mutation, and mutations are usually recessive and do sometimes skip a generation. But we didn't learn in school what makes the hair color turn on—or off. Now we know that red hair is attributed to a loss of function mutation and, at some point, this knowledge will be tucked into the curriculum of genetics. But the story of red hair is unlikely to appear alongside it in textbooks. That's not how science works; the pursuit of pure knowledge attempts to put aside myth and bias. And maybe that's too bad. Because when the scientists, including Harding, went hunting in the genome for the human connection to a pigmentary mutation, they not only found its mechanism, but they also associated themselves with the tale of an epic gene.

Walking away from Harding's office, I am suffused with the deepest sense of wonder. Seeing the science, knowing when red hair emerged as well as its scarcity, erased any doubt that the ancient associations were based on observable redheads. Of course the Neanderthal thing is absurd, but the timing is not. At around fifty thousand years old, we are relatively new to the planet, but redheads are certifiably old enough to have been included in story and song from the first. Redheads are a variant that survived, a color minority, though not a skin color precisely, not a race, but still subject to identification by the wary eyes and wagging tongues of the majority.

I can't help thinking: Am I related in some traceable way to all redheads, if there were any such genetic thing as "all redheads"? And I wonder how Harding can be studying something so primal to me and be utterly uninterested in its expression, in the hair itself. Does her genotype make her intellectually uninterested in my phenotype?

Wandering in and out of the lush gardens of Oxford, and up and down the Carfax Tower, getting some tea, looking in shops along the small streets, I end up at the Ashmolean Museum. Founded in 1683, it is Britain's oldest public museum, and one of the oldest in the world. Passing great antiquities, whole tapestries, stuff I can't name, barely noticing, I am trying to understand the sequencing of the gene—the math that takes it backward in time to the chimps and then forward again, mutating, rolling luxuriatingly and exquisitely amid the ladder of the double helix. Eventually I find myself standing in front of the painting *Gentle Spring* by Anthony Frederick Sandys. Dated 1865, Sandys's painting, oil on canvas, was accompanied in its first exhibition by a sonnet by Algernon Charles Swinburne, inspired by the picture. I am reading the signage to myself, trying to pay attention, while what looks like Persephone comes into focus in the frame in full Pre-Raphaelite splendor: the requisite red hair, the odd truthfulness hinting at both the light of day and the impending gloom of night; poppies, indicating sleep and death in the background, almost overshadowed by this sturdy woman, her wide, high breasts, crisscrossed with the piping of her diaphanous gown, pink nipples peeping through the fabric. I am looking at someone I know well, looking at me, looking at her through a see-through dress.

Her hair is gathered up, sort of Grecian, kind of German, coiled atop her head, with flowers tucked into it. I've done that many times, parting it in the back and winding it until it rolled like sleeping snakes on either side, then pinning them to my crown, tucking new buds within the coils. She has gathered flowers in the folds of her dress, holding the resulting swag with her pale hands, white as her bare feet; I use the front of my blouse, out there in the dew in the morning, barefoot, in the garden, with flowers or fruit or any of the bounty of the early day.

On the first Christmas morning of my new marriage, it was carrots pulled from the snow, carried back in the billows of my nightgown while my sweet husband slept upstairs; echoing the theme of our wedding day, on which a sonnet by Edna St. Vincent Millay—a redhead—was read about giving love, like apples bouncing in a shirt, saying "Look, what I have and these are all for you!"

The image on the canvas echoes something, repeating some ancient theme in my head, familiar and distant but moving in on me. Looking around, I feel suffused by the mnemonic of my own sexual identity, reminded of how that identity is indistinguishable from my self, as much an aspect of me as my hair and my skin. It is my hair and skin and attitude and intelligence. Any effort made to elevate the story of red hair away from those themes and place it solely in scientific hands will fail. Looking at this almost naked redhead, I know for certain that hers is the skin that will not be shed, this identical existence, this sexualized woman. The proximity of Persephone to Harding's lab makes me laugh aloud in the museum.

And while we are witnessing one another, the experience shifts back to the deeply personal, as no less than this vibrant wife of Hades himself is thus choosing to show anyone who is looking what is under my drab reporter's clothes, my blazer, gray trousers, and loafers. The sheer colors that bond us to one another are being peekabooed through Persephone's shift, radiating right through her garment, off the canvas, with a power that is palpable. And there we stand, looking at one another, the reporter and Persephone, a metaphor of science and art, and I am the only one blushing.

Later, as I pack up my things to move on to interview the next scientist, I am beginning to think that science can do nothing to extinguish the fiery tale of red hair.

That desire is primal is without dispute. Hardwired in us, the love of the chase is ancient and biological, reenacted on street corners, in elevators, and even at the gym. Though the arousal associated with adolescence is spontaneous, appearing with the onset of hormones, as we age, we identify images outside ourselves to stimulate our desires. And we pursue them. We must, because if not for one person pursuing another, none of us would be here. Ultimately, desire is nothing without its object, and much like the story of red hair, its genetics are only part of an epic tale. You cannot tell the story of one without the other.

I like to play a game with myself when traveling. I call it "Who Are They?"

I pick a tiny category like clothes, or some mornings shoes, or occasionally haircuts, lapel size, or ties, and try to determine which country each person I pass is from based on it.

Is it bias?

You bet. It's riddled with bias, class, culture, this odd game I play. I am drawn to it by a sense of wonder I have when in a place of any international mix. I lapse into it the instant I set foot off a plane nearly anywhere but in America.

Two days after meeting Harding at Oxford, I am walking in Edinburgh to meet the man who discovered the gene for red hair in humans. But first I have to find Lauriston Place. After a few minutes, the game shifts slightly as I move uphill through a sea of students and tourists. Student, student, student. Tourist, student, tourist, student. Local. Local. And soon I am counting three students, four tourists, three locals. And then splitting off within the locals, tallying one in four, five in ten, then one, two, three, four, five redheads in a row. There are redheads everywhere. I have never had this experience. I have, instead, been the only white person in thousands of shoppers in East Africa on market day, the only redhead I saw for days on end in China, the only redhead in the room countless times everywhere else in the world.

Notebook out, I have three tallies going at once. Four in ten, five in ten, six in ten, grouping people by color. Five in ten. Three of them tall. This is like swimming in a school of me. A small school, perhaps, but one so obvious and delightful that I am giggling. There are redheads on the street, in shops, in cars. There are redheads riding by in the double-decker bus. Scribbling in my notebook, I am interrupted by a small, light-haired woman, probably French, who asks me for directions, and the joke's on me since to her, I look like a local.

Jonathan Rees is thinking the same thing I am, that I am judgmental. He's not at all surprised by my tally marks, my game, when I show it to him in his office.

"Humans are obsessed with appearance," he says. "We politely tiptoe around that, of course, but then we'll say, 'Did you have a late night last night?' looking into the face of a colleague, making a judgment. I'm amazed how much my brain is estimating every minute I walk down the street—how much attention we spend on it. We underestimate our fascination with it all."

Not all of us. Certainly not Rees. He torqued it into a major career move.

After reading Roger Cone's paper in which there was that tantalizing suggestion about the role the red-haired marker in mice might play in human pigmentation, Rees knew that the gene was there, waiting for someone to discover it. And, he knew, humans being what we are, that few would try. It's the nature of us, he thinks, that as fascinated as we may be with each other's looks—"Only other people are vain," he clarifies, with a flat-line smile—we know frustratingly little about the science behind those traits that govern how we look. At the time of our interview, there still appears little, if any, interest in any genes for a hair color other than red.

Intrigued by Cone's work, Rees put together a team to look for the gene in humans, and they found not one but several different MC1R variants. Comparisons between the human and the chimpanzee showed that the gene for red hair was stable while in Africa; that is, there was evidence of strong selection against skin lightening or change in hair color to red. Simply put, the gene was not allowed to diversify. But once humans moved out of Africa, the red hair gene went a bit wild, and in non-African populations, particularly in Europe, many different mutations appeared, leaving us a spectrum of redheads. Someone with very bright red hair will have little eumelanin (brown/black) but lots of phaeomelanin (red/yellow) and is much more likely to carry two different copies of the gene than, say, a strawberry blond. And this differentiation will have a tremendous impact on their skin. People who carry only one changed allele—whether or not they have red hair—tend to burn more easily and are more prone to large numbers of freckles. It turns out that the MC1R gene encodes a receptor that, in turn, is expressed on the pigment of skin cells (melanocytes) and reacts to a hormone that activates the production of eumelanin, the dark pigment. Inactivate the receptor and phaeomelanin will accumulate in the pigment cells and result in fair skin and red hair.

And so it was the very diversity of the gene—its varieties, each perhaps with its own special survival mechanism—that allowed Rees's team to date the red hair mutations and look for evidence of natural selection, the principle described by Charles Darwin in *On the Origin of Species*, under which "each slight variation, if useful, is preserved."

Walking through Edinburgh might suggest to the naïve observer that red hair must be very useful, indeed. There are so many of us here. And I say so to Rees as he closes his office door while offering me a cup of tea as well as a little gossip about his secretary, Karen.

"Not really a blonde," he says, nodding in her direction. This isn't surprising. There are so few real blondes in the world.

"A redhead."

"What?" I spill hot tea on my trousers. I have never in my life heard of anyone bleaching out red hair.

Rees gives me a knowing nod, leaving me to run the odds that the man who has run his hands over more redheads than possibly any man in history could share an office with a woman who has banished hers. And in a country where the color is more common than anywhere else in the world, it brings up the question of the value of red hair. What's it worth? During all my research into red hair, I have been betting that there is some advantage to this color. Whatever purpose red hair truly serves, it must have some evolutionary value, or what is known to scientists as the "biologically materialistic position." Or does it?

To date, red hair has spread to only perhaps 4 percent of the world's population, despite the density in pockets such as the United Kingdom, the Republic of Ireland, and Australia. About 10 percent of the U.K. population is redhaired, although Rees estimates that as many as 40 percent of Scots carry the gene. In America only about 2 percent of the population has red hair; only 0.03 percent of the French are red-haired.

Certainly redheads are an example of the principles of biological evolution—mutation, selection of some sort, isolation, migration, and drift—since they appeared as a pigmentary variation of the human genetic code, and, for the most part, isolated themselves in pockets of contained landmasses and survived. The mapping of the human genome has proven that humans are 99.9 percent genetically identical, which theoretically, at least, should diminish the importance of our outward differences. Ultimately, widespread understanding and acceptance of the genome might erase our need to see ourselves separated by race.

But what about by trait, I wonder. The visible patterns of human variation are embedded with heritages that allow us to understand our history not only collectively but also individually, one person at a time. And it is here that science seems to lose its footing, when attempting to overtake the persistence of myth. While science provides the single root of us all by directing us toward our ancestry, our individual identities depend on our ability to tell ourselves apart. Even when seeking another human as a partner, each of us brings these separate identities, attempting to successfully hawk our heritages in the marketplace of mating. Having walked among so many of my own just minutes before, it is possible to imagine that the most successful peddler of the trait of red hair is the story of the hair color itself.

But I don't say that to Rees. These are not questions I expect him to answer. He's got his own trouble. Unfortunately, red hair does not lend itself either to a single classification (as "red hair") or to easy agreement on the shades within the color. This presents a major obstacle to research. And his is not the first investigation into the color to be frustrated by this constraint. The question of what exactly red hair is has troubled many good scientists who have tried to study it. In a 1952 paper entitled "Red Hair Colour as a Genetical Character," T. E. Reed bemoans the fact that to that date, "the problem of defining what is meant by 'red hair,' is one of considerable difficulty," and describes various methods used in attempts to measure the color. These include a particularly curious effort in which the Hardy recording spectrophotometer at the National Physical Laboratory in Teddington, England, was used to gauge the percentage of recorded light from each specimen of hair investigated, "relative to a magnesium oxide standard." In the end, Reed concludes that "a better method for classifying red hair is needed in order to use it as a genetical marker." Despite being published in *The Annals of Eugenics*, more than half a century ago, Reed's paper is still cited in contemporary work, including that of Professor Rees, offering a solid demonstration of how little work has been done in the field of pigmentary genetics, particularly that of hair.

According to Dr. Rees, even today no two scientists can agree on what to call the various shades and, as a result, no single rating scale has been established to consistently and accurately describe the observable characteristics for each type of red hair: strawberry blond, auburn, ginger, carrot, and so on. Even under the microscope, the hair color's response to light eludes much more than a gross division between dark and light, where one person's strawberry blond becomes another's light red. And in science, accuracy rules.

To illustrate, I ask Rees to classify me.

"Pale skin," he says. "Reddish hair. Is it dyed?"

My instinct to slap him must show on my face because he immediately shoves both hands into opposite armpits and caves as far back into his chair as he can, saying, "Terrible about dye. Get fooled all the time. Usual man that I don't notice things. Blokes say, 'She's not a natural blonde,' I say, 'How do you know?' It's hard to look at people in a systematic way. We're all guilty of being incredibly selective when we're trying to be incredibly rigorous."

It comes out all in a rush, his hands still jammed, and it's kind of charming, in a nutty-professor kind of way. This quality of respectful humility must be a great boon when he approaches redheads on the street and asks them to come up to his lab to volunteer for a little scientific study.

Why did I want to slap him, anyway? What possible reactive inclination is it that makes me defensive about how I look? Simple vanity?

"Vanity is more hardwired than many think," he says, relaxing only slightly. How attached we are to our vanity is something to consider, he says, and is a worthwhile subject in itself, especially if it injects "a little more biology" into our maunderings about physical appearance. And with that, we break for lunch and I go to some restaurant where, looking up into the face of the waitress named Ramune, I am gazing into the exact face of my dear friend Mary Elizabeth, co–witch camper. I don't mean they just look alike; I mean she has the exact same face, right down to the cleft at the tip of her nose. And her posture. Though not her hands; Mary Elizabeth has broad nails. But the chin, the nose, the flare of the cheekbones, the long throat, erect posture, and broad forehead. It's breathtaking. I wonder if Ramune can arch one eyebrow like Mary Elizabeth. I guess I'll soon find out if I keep staring.

I have also noticed several versions of my friend Jack here in Edinburgh. Jack is tall, big-boned, pale, with light red hair, and looks like he came out of central casting to play a berserk Danish Viking.

Taking the suggestion of Dr. Rees to infuse my musings about physical appearance with some biology, I realize that my selections are local versions of faces that are well known to me. These familiar physiognomies are also in familiar company to one another. With their white skin and ruddy coloring, these are faces we traditionally associate with the Scottish. Redheads thrive in Scotland's climate, not because the climate produces them but because the variation of reddish hair and light skin already existed in all of them, and nature, in turn, selected for the most suitable variation. This variation existed in them because while the melano-cortin receptor gene is invariant among Africans, resulting in enormous natural selection against the red-haired, light-skinned mutation in that gene, among Europeans and Asians, the variable characteristic for the red-haired gene allows for it to be selected.

The greatest danger to redheads lies in living on the equator, where the burning rays of the noonday sun prevent them from doing the business of hunting, gathering, and farming. There, the skin of redheads burns quickly, while in the more northern climates, like Scotland, the pale skin that travels with the hair color became a genetic advantage, letting in more sunlight and preventing a deficiency of vitamin D. In its extreme, such a deficiency would promote rickets, a bone-softening condition that in women compro-mises pelvic strength and inhibits childbirth.

What the MC1R offers in humans is balance between the choice of the hues black/brown and yellow/red. The mutation is in the gene that encodes the receptor; the receptor controls the balance of the different types of pigment. And through the inheritance of this mutation travels the trait of red hair. But of the color itself and its materialistic worth, it might be much like the peacock's tail, little more than a flamboyant display in the eyes of the beholder, a flash to attract but lacking in any other advantage unto itself.

Outside the laboratory it is awkward to talk about skin. When we do, we communicate in little more than the language we've been carefully taught. By contrast, inside Rees's lab, it was easy to talk phenotype.

"Eunuchs have great skin," Rees tells me as we resume our interview.

I guess he would know. A dermatologist by training and practice, Rees is what he describes as a "jobbing doctor," a clinical academic. "Half a doctor, half clinician," he explains. Pleased at the prospect of studying our own genetic inheritance, he took to it, he tells me, because human evolution is the greatest story in history. Before turning to hair color, his research had been pretty much limited to itch.

"Itch?" I ask, probably feigning interest badly.

"Itch is a nice thing," he says as one hand tucks into an armpit and the other musses the receding hair on top of his head. Talking to a reporter must make him itchy; he's in motion in the chair the whole time we are together. "When you go to the dermatologist, the one thing that you can say to make them go under their desk is 'I'm itchy.'"

Setting out to measure itch, Rees strapped devices to people who reported itch and recorded the number of scratches in a time period, while people slept, thereby verifying their testimony on infrared videos. His goal was to establish "an objective measurement of itch," and when he was done with that research, he began to struggle with an objective measurement of differences in the ability of people to tan, which required him to get a whole lot of people to let him "shine light on their bums."

And he's looking right at me. Am I supposed to volunteer for this?

We agree that, in the interest of journalism, shining some ultraviolet light on the inside of my forearm would be fine and that a blood test to sequence my gene for red hair would be in order, as well, but that no, shining any light on my bum—mostly because I'm not positive just where that is—is out. That I can ask the man to justify his life's work, but not if my "bum" is my butt, is a reminder to me that most things contain their own neutralizer, their personal vaccine: getting the facts without crossing some lines, for instance. And on the way up the stairs to the workup room, this idea broadens. Sickle-cell anemia gives its carriers a resistance to malaria. Eunuchs apparently have great skin. Redheads have pale skin, making me wonder if there is a type of assortive mating involved. If the lightness of skin is the thing that is valued by a potential mate, perhaps you get the hair in the bargain. Maybe the delicate shade of skin is perceived as some kind of reward, or at least was considered so from time to time in our human history. For some people, the erubescence of the redhead might be the kind of stimulus for which no throttle exists.

Before I left for England, I interviewed people I know who have what we popularly consider a "weakness" for redheads, the foremost among them being a male friend whose dating career establishes him as a serial monogamist of the red-haired, a regular ordinal polygamist of the color. Even in the strictest terms, he qualifies as an expert. My friend Nicky defines his lifelong pursuit of redheads as both a weakness and a passion. When he finally married at forty-nine, it was to a redhead of astonishing beauty.

"What is it?" I had asked.

Delighted to offer a synopsis of his knowledge, he replied, "They are the only women in the world whose orgasm you can actually see," he said. "The pale skin, the blood flushing the chest, rising up the throat, and rushing into the face. There is nothing like it in the world."

For any reasonable man, the response would be sufficient payout, a sort of at-home biofeedback calculation of one's genuine sexual performance. It amused me to recast it under the lens of another quote of Dryden's I had been toting around, looking for a place to use it. In his 1697 *Alexander's Feast*, the poet wrote, "None but the brave deserves the fair," hinting at trophy aspects of the pale skin in some parts of the world. When you take a redhead to bed, you take it all: the skin, the hair, the centuries of fear and loathing, all tumbled into one, all requiring a determined courage to consummate the forbidden fruit of your labors.

Not wanting to frighten Dr. Rees again, I don't mention Nicky and the observation he offered on redheads and orgasm. Or Dryden. Remembering our first phone conversation all those months ago, during which he suggested I read the press he'd gotten, those clips including all the references to sex, I realize he has not once invoked those sexualized images while explaining his work. Right up to this moment, he has told me a little gossip, but no tales, and I don't want to sway him in that direction. He sticks to science. I stick out my arm to give blood, noticing, not for the first time, that I have no freckles there, on its underside, and that the skin is as pale a shade as I have on my body, one that allows for the blue of the underlying veins to radiate through. It's smooth there, as well, looking less spoiled by the sun and the elements than the skin on my nose or chest. It seems untouched and really quite lovely to behold. To my near horror, it is there that Dr. Rees plans to radiate me with three varying strengths of light, one of which, at least, I am left to assume, will burn this skin. Sun always has.

Through his work on red hair, Rees studies the skin's susceptibility to the sun. And for redheads, this is not a pretty picture, since all carriers of the mutation that results in red hair—even those who do not exhibit the hair color— are more at risk for skin cancer. This includes melanoma, which kills 20 percent of its victims, making the MC1R the major susceptibility site for the most common cancer in Caucasians. It is not yet clear why.

As good a discovery as it is, the MC1R has not untangled the influence of genetics from that of the environment. Consider the fact that the risk of developing skin cancer within any random sample of humanity varies more than a hundredfold. Ask an epidemiologist about the incidence and prevalence of developing the disease and he or she might tell you that the kind of light Dr. Rees is shining on my arm is the major determining factor. Ask a geneticist, and he or she might say it's my pigment. Rees reminds me that they are both right.

Along with taking my blood and burning my skin, Rees would like me to see some mice. And so, bandaged from my blood test, I travel across Edinburgh to another lab, only to find that the man in charge wants me to take a shower. It's adding up to be one of those days as a reporter, I guess: give blood, get zapped by ultraviolet light, get wet.

Rees had made an e-mail introduction between Professor Ian Jackson and me when I was still back home. It didn't prepare me for the phenotype twenty-first-century space pirate: gold hoop earring, the lenses of his glasses floating over his face within a mere gesture of a frame, a watch with all internal workings pulsing under a petri dish of a crystal. Then, Jackson moves, and that is the last still image of him I will get. Stretching to three, four steps at a time, he climbs up, up, up, and I am perpetually at his calf level, following him in what's beginning to feel like the riggings of his lab, as he talks me into taking a shower to protect the sterility of the lab.

We are at the Medical Research Council, Human Genetics Unit (MRCHGU), and he offers only, "This is a rabies-free island," in explanation, as he dodges into an office to check the score of the World Cup, back out through a series of rooms, and down a labyrinth of stairs. Rees described Jackson as someone who "goes running with a drinking club, or drinking with a running club," the repetition of which brings a clarification whisked over Jackson's shoulder: "It's a drinking club with a running problem." One of those people on the extreme end of extreme sports, someone who runs literally for days, sometimes in boots, up mountains, he is another species, not my own.

We are in a basement now, the floor is wet everywhere, and we are looking at fish as he characterizes what he, a senior scientist at the MRCHGU, does for a living. "I make a model of what the world is like and go test it," he says.

And with that, he is off and I am looking at tanks of zebra fish, wondering how they fit into Jackson's model of a red-haired world, when Darren Logan, the graduate student with whom Jackson has temporarily parked me, pipes in. "Nonmammalian melanocortin receptors," he says.

Zebra fish are a model organism in the laboratory, especially if you are studying pigmentation, as their vibrantly colored horizontal stripes display some of the wonder of color itself. Zebra fish conveniently have transparent and externally developing embryos and reach reproductive maturity in approximately six weeks, so an observer can not only watch the color form but can also do so over a short period of time.

Logan whips through millions of years of pigmentary genetics in a minute, explaining that any animal with color has melanin. What he wants to know is how far back in the vertebrate lineage the mutation allowing for red hair emerged.

"Fish. Fugu. Tetraodon. Sea squirt. Flies, worms," he says, sliding further from humans with each reference. And I had been happy that my ancestors didn't resemble Neanderthals. Now I'm seeing fins and bubbles.

"The most dramatic thing we see, about anything, is its color," he says, staring as the pigments in the form of fish ripple by. "It's the way we describe each other, our striking feature, and it will be so wonderful when it's irrelevant to our human beingness."

Irrelevant? Watching him watch the fish, I think about the physiognomics and the connections made thousands of years ago, linking the color and character of animals with those of man. I ask Logan what he thinks about human redheads.

"They are scientific things," he shrugs. "Just another gene to me."

And just like that, Jackson reappears and we are off again, apparently not to the showers. The plan has changed. If I'll just suit up, it will be fine. On a rabies-free island, within this mouse lab, suiting up in the locker room, I am about to enter an ever more sterile concentric circle, though the idea does nothing to focus my view. Haunted by the idea of the potential irrelevance of color, I look at the cages and cages of mice, stacked and classified and well cared for. In their bloodlines is a heritage that extends from steppes to house to Asia to here, which means that through all that, and through our genes, we are connected. Their story is part of my own as well as Jackson's, whose phenotype includes a hair color that is lighter than strawberry blond. I wonder if, like his researcher studying the fish, and like Harding, who gave the date to the gene, he draws the line at the laboratory door, leaving the story on the other side. I ask him about his genotype.

"Red-haired mother," he says, proudly. "I knew you'd be one when you first called," he says through his mask and under his hairnet. Neither one of us can see the connection at this moment, but it's there and he adds, nodding, "I figured it was what got you interested in the tale," implying that it is part of his interest, as well. And I'm about to ask when he sweeps back out of the mouse room while telling me about a cousin's recent wedding. During the reception he moved from table to table, asking all the relatives to spit in the tubes he'd brought with him. Having successfully collected his family's genetic material, he took it back to the lab where he sequenced their genetic changes for the mutation for red hair.

*　　*　　*

On my last morning of interviews, I am back at Rees's lab and notice for the first time the poster on the clinic's waiting room wall.

WANTED

Red and ALIVE

Persons with red, brown or blonde hair

Families and twins

REWARD

Will be the satisfaction of helping
with important skin research

We are trying to find reasons for why some people's
skin is more sensitive than others to sunlight
and other substances

CONTACT

536–2044

"The public information office cooks those up," Rees says. "Middle-aged professor seeks redheads. Sort of thing works well. Brings them in a bit," he adds, as he checks my UV exposure spots, which, despite my fears of burning, show only minimal amounts of red on all three. He tells me that my blood will go off to the lab to be sequenced and that the results will be back by e-mail in a few weeks. After that, not only will he have another hit for his database, but also I will know just what kind of redhead I am.

I might be homozygous, meaning that both copies of the gene are nonfunctional. Heterozygotes are mixed. In genetics, the "normal" allele is called the "wild type," referring to the allele found in the majority of a wild population. Most redheads are homozygous for the mutation while heterozygotes are somewhere in between homozygotes and wild-type individuals for skin type, freckling, and shade of hair.

He will not posit on which I may be. Neither does he seem engaged in my remaining questions. Sure, he's heard blush is a big issue for redheads—uncontrollable at times, frequent in incidence, and sometimes embarrassing—but it hasn't been studied so he doesn't give it much credit. There is a story that redheads are more prone to industrial deafness than people of other hair colors, and it "might be true since the melanocytes are there in the middle ear," he says, shrugging. He talks about Job's syndrome, supporting an idea that redheads are more prone to bad infections, and admits there is "lots of woolly data, not at all convincing, claiming red hair predisposes you to something else—irritants, sensitive skin—but we haven't found a difference." I name my sensitivity to detergents, perfumes, and soaps. He shrugs again, but doesn't theorize.

I ask him if he's ever heard of the phrase, born out of the American South, "I'll beat you like a redheaded stepchild." He hasn't but he listens as I explain that it came from the status attached to illegitimate offspring with the white master. He smiles politely but shakes his head and I think that he, too, sees only the science and little of the story, until he offers that he has heard that "Romans paid higher sums for their red-haired slaves" and that at one point in time "Brahmins were forbidden to marry redheads." And my head pops up from my notebook. He's telling tales.

"Oh, it has never been neutral," he says, when asked about the hair color's value vis-à-vis its genetic story, suggesting that one equally drives the other and adding that whatever its merits, the willing choice of mate based on appearance—whether this appearance be thought highly sexy, simply pecuniary, or strictly forbidden—"may some day prove important in human history."

Maybe it already has. Walking along the street back to my hotel to pack and then leave Edinburgh, I immediately start counting again. I stop in a tea shop and of the eight people inside three are redheads. Out on the street again, the first two people to walk by are redheads. Thirty seconds later, another redhead walks by. Eighteen seconds later another one. I don't expect to ever be in another place like this.

And then I am caught behind a strolling couple and can't see past them. They are maybe in their twenties; they are moving languidly down the street, holding hands until he releases hers and drops back a half a step or so behind her. He's reaching out—what is he doing? Is he trying to stroke away a bee behind her head? I cross the street and watch as he is softly stroking her hair, talking to her, walking a full pace behind her now, talking, reaching out behind her, almost hovering, looking adoringly at the back of her head, running his hand ever so lightly once, twice, over her golden red curls.

Digestif

Recipe for One Redhead

MY MOTHER DIDN'T cook, didn't leave behind a box of recipes. She did other memorable things, though. Like brushing her hair while telling me the secret of life.

When I was eight, we were in her bedroom one evening and the steam from the bathtub she had just left was ghosting past me, through my view of her. She was sitting, damp and lovely, at her vanity table; the dark purple taffeta skirt intimating her chorus-girl knees like a matinee curtain.

I had recently cut out two hunks of my red bangs, leaving me with a jack-o'-lantern forehead. Accenting that, I was also missing the teeth on either side of the front ones, and the exquisite agony of shoving my tongue in and out of the open spots ached almost as much as the longing I had to be as she was: serene, idly brushing my hair, and old enough to emit wisdom.

"You know," she said, not looking at me, but gazing at herself in the triptych mirror. "The world of women is divided into two categories."

Here it came. The Rosetta stone. The knowledge upon which I could build a life. And I was so ready I sat down.

"Those who believe Rhett Butler came back," she said, languidly. "And those who don't care."

It was—it remains—about as useful as an oyster fork: ornamental and amusing but hardly a delivery system of knowledge. But in that, she is the perfect foil, my carrier, bringing something to the table whether she knew it or not.

My father knew what he brought to the table. It was easy for anyone to see: He was a redhead. My mother, though born a brunette, was epically sexy and supplied for me the stories, the anecdotes on the powers of persuasion of women, the captions to what I was supposed to read under the visual stimuli provided by man. This is where they braid in my personal heritage: my father bringing the look, and my mother, the sex, to my story.

She told me many things while brushing her lovely hair. And I always listened and watched and watched and listened and the image and the lesson travel together like truth and myth, like the science of red hair and the folklore of its sexual power, like alleles.

PART THREE

SEX

CHAPTER SIX

The Palette of the Succubus

*On Satan the Color Red Is One Thing;
on Women, It Is Altogether Another*

"ALL THE KICK-ASS girls have red hair," said Herve St. Louis, matter-of-factly. When St. Louis got schooled in sequential art, he was told three things: First, it's called sequential art, not comics; second, there are rules; third, one of those rules is that all the kick-ass girls are redheads.

St. Louis lives in Montreal and runs a Web site, Toondoctor.com, a hub for people who want to know about animation and digital graphics, which is where I tracked him down, asking him, among other things, to expand on that "kick-ass" thing. He laughed.

"All the action adventure girls have red hair," he said. "Whenever it is an independent girl, not a sidekick person, when she has her own mind, or does as good as the guys, she has red hair."

The rule also appears to apply to the big screen: Ariel in

The Little Mermaid, for instance, not to mention Jessica Rabbit of *Who Framed Roger Rabbit* fame. Both gorgeous, both redheads, both knowing what they want and kicking some serious ass to get it.

"Oh, yeah," St. Louis said. "Blonds are the girlfriend, brunette is the femme fatale, but the heroine, she's the redheaded girl."

For instance?

Josie and the Pussycats, he said, not taking a beat. "Not like Betty and Veronique, who are tied romantically to Archie, who also has red hair, of course. Josie is his counterpart—kind of independent, more than Betty and the black-haired girl. She is not a sidekick; they probably know each other but they are not tied. She has her own comic strip and is independent.

"How about Fifi Brin d'Acier?" he asked, and noting my blankness, added, "Fifi Pinstripes, I think you call it. Two braids sticking out, super strength?" This was sounding familiar.

Pippi Longstocking: My main girl when growing up, I admitted, and now realized, is a (junior-model) kick-ass girl. And a redhead. You bet.

"Lifelong readers pick up the rules," he added. And I did: Starting life as a Pippi, never becoming a Veronica—or, as St. Louis says it, Veronique—being more than a Betty, latching onto Josie the first time I saw her. In my mind, I reconnected my own iconic string of strong, cartooned female redheads, one after the other, right up to Brenda Starr, star reporter of the *Flash*.

At thirteen years old—after years of Pippi and Josie—my dream of the perfect red-haired female was realized in Brenda Starr: The vivid flamboyance of her coiffure, her thrilling job, and her va-voom figure. I was in love with her identity. Gorgeous, intelligent and totally sexual, her kick-ass quality is the integrity she brings every day to readers of the *Star*. A high-octane redhead, Brenda pursued a career, steamy love affairs and good friendships with the same voracious appetite; always on deadline, she wrote clean copy, loved and was loved, and dispensed good advice to her pals. The whole package that is her unblushing self has emblazoned the funny pages continuously since 1940. The creation of Dale Messick, who drew the strip for forty years and then turned over the job to other women to continue, Brenda Starr remains a soap opera, comic strip career dame with mystery, glamour, and, oh, that 1976 marriage (following thirty-six years of dating) to Basil St. John. In the vernacular of magazine headlines, she has it all—something women can have in a cartoon universe. The strip's syndicator, Tribune Media Services, produces a fact sheet that lists Brenda's "ethnic origin," simply as "Red Head."

In the paint box of contemporary cartoonists, red-haired females are flamboyant color icons whose identity carries a hint of the history of the harlot. But in this modern art form, their identity stops right at the brink of minx and goes no further; powerful in her sexiness and sexy in her power, she teeters on the cusp of the hussy but never slips over the edge. It's a great act: The threat of harlotry is always there and yet she never goes directly to it.

By comparison, the small pack of red-haired cartoon character males includes Archie, who is characterized not only by that universally unattractive inability to choose between his girlfriends but also by his ultimate power over them both through this very indecision. In another series, there exists the red-haired Daredevil, who is fabulously powerful though tragically blinded. While both these guys have power, they lack sexuality as an identifying trait.

What appears to have happened is a form of extreme makeover of the red-haired woman, one that was drawn on her good bones but left her darker circles behind. Contemporary fiction writers recognize this and build on the strong, existing themes of redheads' power of desirability to bring us fully dimensional red-haired women, not all of whom merely buck like goats, as portrayed by James Joyce's Buck Mulligan. In "Ode to Redheads," Tom Robbins asks, "Why are your curls the same shade as heartbreak?" Carl Sandburg requests us to "Shake back your hair, O red-headed girl," stating that, "Around and around go ten thousand men hunting a red-headed girl with two freckles on her chin."

Red-haired women are similarly depicted in song lyrics. Billy Joel sings that he thought he was "Duke of Earl when I made it with a red-haired girl in a Chevrolet," and Doc Watson twangs that he's "got a red-haired gal make a hound dog lose his trail."

But it is Bruce Springsteen who rules, married as he is to one of the coolest redheaded women on the planet, Patti Scialfa, backup singer and guitar player in the E Street Band, and mother of their three children. In "Red Headed Woman," he stridently declares the iconography updated, clarifying for the listener that they have "big green eyes that look like, son, they can see every cheap thing that you ever done. Well I don't care how many girls you've dated, man. But you ain't lived til you've had your tires rotated by a redheaded woman."

With their long-standing reputation as highly sexualized

daughters of the devil, how in the world did red-haired women ever get to this place?

To logically plot a course from sexpot demon to Bruce Springsteen's triumphantly erotic redhead would require finding women in history—real or mythological—on whose head red hair is sexual, as well as powerful, but not evil. Without those women as evidence, little can account for the massive revisionism required for this modern tilt toward the sexy-powerful redhead identity and away from the historic evil persona.

A Russian proverb warns us, "There was never a saint with red hair." That's wrong: There's Mary Magdalene, a saint, as well as a controversial biblical figure. Little about her can be agreed upon except that she has reformed from something. In the sixth century, the Catholic church officially made various women in the Bible—only some of them Marys—into a single Mary Magdalene and ascribed to her the sinful qualities described in Luke as well as the description of the woman from whom seven evil spirits were ejected. This last bit suggests that Mary may have come by her red hair via the same route as Cain, Esau, and David: through her association with the devil.

But in 1969, a Catholic church decree again separated the various incorrectly fused biblical women from one another—the prostitute, the one possessed by seven devils, a sinner who washed Jesus' feet and dried them with her hair, another who only washed his feet, the one from whom seven devils were ejected—but did little to part Mary Magdalene from her identity. By this time she had been firmly established as the patron saint of fallen women and, in this role, her identity remains braided to an ideal of repentant sexuality. In this role she not only serves as a poster girl for that fine line between good and evil, but also illustrates the confused relationship Christians have with hair.

Christians have made themselves a regular bed of nails on which to rest their feelings about hair: something utilitarian but not at all comfortable. We are instructed in the Bible that a woman's long hair is a glory to her because it can be used as a covering (I Corinthians 11:15) but also that it is an object that invites desire (Song of Solomon 4:1). Desire is a funky thing in a religion where the two principal characters—Jesus and his mother—are both virgins. But it is this unsettled sense we have of hair that has made Mary Magdalene a wonderful draw for painters for centuries.

Titian painted her several times in the sixteenth century, always enshrouded in her long red hair. Dante Gabriel Rossetti, in an 1857 watercolor, depicted her with unbound red hair falling down around her, hiding her former self— or, some say exhibiting her true self—a kind of moralistic peekaboo behind a head of hair which nowhere in the Bible is described as red. And yet, in art, Mary Magdalene is positively adorned in erubescent tresses.

Portrayed as everything from the holy harlot to a shriveled, withered, postsexual woman (in Donatello's 1455 painted wood statue), Mary Magdalene's most compelling role is under that weight of red hair, which titillates both the saintly and the sinning qualities in us all. Somehow, it does so without making us decide which of those qualities red hair represents, instead providing the ultimate existential relief: Even sinners can be saints, and saints can be sinners. On the head of Mary Magdalene, things take a decided turn for the better for the red-haired female, seeming to achieve, at the very least, a flat plane between good and evil.

But if Mary Magdalene's hair color is the level spot, the proverbial balanced book on the head that comes as a result of perfect posturing, what immediately preceded her? From what image of the red-haired female does she spring or evolve? Moving backward in time from the portrayals of Mary Magdalene by Rossetti, Titian, and Donatello, we are searching for female redheads in art whose color had yet to teeter on the evil-good fulcrum, those who were still purely tipped down into evil and, going back perhaps a bit too far, hit upon a place where color almost completely disappeared.

Despite his flamboyant redness, his incarmined offspring and the sometimes bloody termination of his marriages, Henry VIII inaugurated a certain colorlessness. It erupted in the 1520s and '30s, with the revolution that would break England from the Catholic church and, after some turmoil, turn it into a Protestant state. Amid this tumult arose the perception that color was Catholic. Catholics were idolaters with their rosary beads and the relics of saints. In the fervor of the times, all things papal were not considered Protestant and were therefore anti-Christ, and so the use of any but the most necessary color was eventually banned within the churches of England.

Looking for a live version of this idea, I went to St. Paul's, the massive Christopher Wren–designed cathedral along the Thames in London. It is not the first Christian edifice to occupy the spot. Its immediate predecessor, old St. Paul's, was consecrated in 1240, expanded by Inigo Jones in the 1630s and '40s, and then burnt to the ground in the Great Fire of 1666. The present structure was built between 1675 and 1710 and while its decoration has a checkered history, it was originally—and for a long time after—laid out in shades of gray.

Christopher Wren had lost control of the completion of his marvelous wonder in 1710 and was finally dismissed for political reasons. But he originally envisioned decoration that included beautifying the inside of the cupola with colorful mosaics along the lines of those in St. Peter's in Rome. His logic, it seems, rested on the durability of the vivid color of mosaics. With paint, the sooty, filthy air of London would do quick work, he realized, reducing any mere paint to gray smears in a short time.

Wren's plans were what is referred to as Carolingian, which pertains to the arts, script, or culture of the Frankish dynasty that reigned in France from C.E. 751 to 987. But the flourishes he envisioned never stood a chance of seeing the light of day under the Church of England of his time. Instead, James Thornhill was commissioned to fresco the cupola of St. Paul's, and between 1716 and 1719, he did so, in monochrome. The goal, two hundred years after Henry VIII, was to continue to distinguish it from the multicolored decoration of continental Roman Catholic churches. Indeed, this disinclination toward colorized adornment constrained any plans for more than shades of gray for nearly another century and a half. Then, in 1872, Queen Victoria attended a service at St. Paul's and declared it to be "the most dreary, dingy, melancholy undevotional church." God praise the queen.

There has been a place of Christian worship on the site of St. Paul's since C.E. 604. Upon entering the great cathedral, I experience an immediate sense of being tucked into some ancient rhythm of worship and barely notice being hustled into a small and determined-looking band of people moving forward toward a set of folding chairs. They sit. I sit. They wait. I ask my neighbor what we are waiting for and he whispers, "evensong," just as a small man in a robe comes down to my new group of friends and says to the twenty or so of us that since we are early, we are invited to sit in the choir. Up we go, up and around and behind and then into the choir stalls carved by Grinling Gibbons, a master woodworker frequently called upon by Wren.

The individual seats are exquisite in dark wood, each high and straight along the back. Slipping quietly into mine, I meditate on the remarkable history within the church and the experience I'd had earlier that same day at Darwin's great house, when an almost unimaginably resplendent sound ascends through my maunderings. There has been a choir of boys and men at the cathedral for more than nine centuries and the very timbre of their voices thrums something primal in even an oblique religious observer like me. The members round a corner, bringing to full force their elegance, and process by, brushing each of us in our box with the light touch of perfection.

Tears surge from my eyes and in trying to tip them back, I look up. And there it is.

Three choir spandrels in the wall before me tell the story of the Fall and the Redemption. In the center spandrel is "Adam in the Garden," his look suggesting he sees what's about to happen. To his right an angel is attempting to thwart Satan, who, in "The Temptation," the right-hand spandrel, is shown in mosaic as a handsome but frightening winged figure. He points to the forbidden fruit with his right hand while gesturing with his left to someone to be silent. It's Eve, naked but for adornment in her golden hair, a gold so preciously metallic that I wonder at its karat—it's so exquisite as to be the envy of any blonde beholding it.

Toward the nave is "The Expulsion," in which the archangel with his sword of light is driving the first couple out of the garden. Adam, a fig leaf now firmly in place, loops his arm over the bent neck of Eve. But the fallen Eve is changed—she's cowering, now, under the weight of her long, red hair.

The story of the Fall is an attempt to account for the sufferings of humans. Resembling other myths about how man and woman came to sin and die, it is unique in its implication that we brought about the Fall through our own free will, by choosing to disobey God's direction against partaking of the tree of knowledge. And in any accounting for how the problems of evil came to fall on the heads of humanity forever after, there would need to be a traceable source, a scapegoat, which is how Eve is portrayed in the mosaics. She is seen carrying the stain of sin—the original sin—much as the red hair of her son Cain will later mark his own fall from grace.

I get it. Sitting under it, looking up, even through my tears, I understand the clear message through its blatant use of color. Good girl to bad girl. Blonde to redhead. Why, I immediately wonder? Not why did they do it: The colorization is as obvious as its inflammatory meaning. But why do I understand it? And why, as it seems, does everyone else understand it, as well? How, exactly, was that understanding ensured?

Look at her—there she is, Eve, the icon for the instant that the sway of the senses descends upon the soul: eating that apple, felling humanity. It's a wonder the fruit ever recovered its status. But Eve never did. From the day she made eye contact with the snake, hers has been a tale of devouring woe. And we get that in the telling and retelling of the tale of the fall from grace. But we get something more in the red-haired portrayal of Eve—which shouts, "Don't miss this!"—as the hair color emblazons itself into the consciousness of the onlooker. Because you might miss the meaning of Eve if you were not observant in any tradition or were a believer in some religion from which you should most assuredly be converted. You might not understand that this is the moment things descended from being heavenly to being merely carnal; the instant when these two godly creations lost their spiritual status and became mere mortals, with all the attending untidy appetites. And, that it's Eve's fault.

Even if you were an observant Christian, you might miss Eve's meaning, since Genesis does not explicitly tell us why the serpent addresses her, even indicating that he may have addressed both members of the first couple. Despite the lack of biblical instruction on this point, both Jewish and Christian tradition choose to present Eve in a very negative light and utilize an identity of gullibility to keep women subservient to men. Not wanting anyone to miss the point of Eve, a simple code is used to ensure that you not only recognize the stain of sin but that you also identify that it is in place on mankind's original object of desire.

Adam, too, has red in his tradition: His very name may be translated as "ruddy," or "earth." And he, too, eats the forbidden fruit. But he never suffers as Eve does, who in both the Jewish and Christian traditions is portrayed in the negative light of her weaknesses. Eve's name is interpreted in the Bible as "the mother of all living," though later rabbinic tradition associates her name with the Aramaic word for "serpent." The Bible's account, in which both Adam and Eve eat of the fruit of the forbidden tree of knowledge, has Adam destined to farm fields of thorns and thistles. But Eve's destiny is to suffer pain in childbirth and, in this, her association to the red-haired Lilith is strong— Lilith's identity becomes defined by her role in bringing about miscarriage and slaying women in pregnancy. Eve does successfully survive her pregnancy, of course, but gives birth to the troubled Cain and Abel, only one of whom ultimately survives, but with both blood on his hands and the devil's mark of red hair on his head.

Looking at the florid mosaic above me, of the portrayal of Eve at the moment things tipped from good to bad, I see that its set piece, its strongest argument, its international language, is its color, the device used to dogmatize its message.

The great mosaics of St. Paul's Cathedral were designed and executed by William Blake Richmond, who had been to the cathedral as a child and, like Queen Victoria, had found it dreary. Later, when learning to see as an artist, he made his first of many trips to Italy in 1859 and eventually was encouraged to publish a book on the Sistine Chapel. He wrote, "I have come to the conclusion that if we are to do good art we must look at Nature through the glass of Titian."

Ah, Titian, the master of sixteenth-century Venetian Renaissance art, the man who asserted the importance of color and applied it vigorously, the painter for whom Titian red was named, braiding forever his name with the golden red-brown that fashionable Venetian women of the time chose to dye their hair. Titian didn't invent the color; he simply copied the trend and immortalized it on canvas.

On a return trip to the Sistine Chapel in 1874, Richmond was able to get up close, finding it encased in scaffolding. But despite hideous vertigo that prevented him from studying the ceiling in minute detail, he got higher than most of us ever get. What he saw was that on the ceiling, in Michelangelo's *Temptation*, a brunette Eve is being handed the apple by a redheaded, bare-breasted serpent-woman, coiled around the tree. In the adjacent fresco, as she is getting thrown out of the garden of Eden, Eve is wearing nothing but a look of shame and a swirl of long red hair.

Commissioned by the fearsome Pope Julius II, the frescoes in Rome depict a way of thinking that reflects back at least as much as it is meant to project a message forward. In art, we borrow, we steal, we imitate, and we lay down rules of representation and call them iconography, sometimes intending the small details to have large influences. In short, iconography is a code for the uneducated as well as a reinforcing identifier for those of us who are illuminated.

When he picked up the brush to paint Eve's hair red, maybe Michelangelo was also picking up the vibrant hue of the "bonfire of the vanities," and the teachings of Girolamo Savonarola, a man to force a reckoning with one's weaknesses. Michelangelo had heard the inflammatory sermons of Savonarola when he was an adolescent, messages that would easily be seared into memory when, in 1497, Savonarola ignited two bonfires, evoking a wrathful God, one whose forgiveness might be had if the people of Florence would part, by fire, with their perfume, books, games, mirrors, and musical instruments. Oh yes, and their wigs.

For images of the kind of fearsome wrath that enflamed Savonarola, you need go no further than back to the Old Testament stories Michelangelo illustrated on the ceiling.

His great biblical depictions range from Adam to Zechariah, stopping in between for the Temptation and Expulsion, the sacrifice of Noah, the Flood and the drunkenness of Noah, running across from altar wall to entrance wall.

Years before, when I had walked under the ceiling of the Sistine Chapel, I was drawn to Eve and to that monstrous snake. Real as well as imagined, the redheads who lure me are on the bad side of the balance sheet: Belle Watley from *Gone with the Wind*. Miss Kitty of *Gunsmoke*. Kiki Roberts, the Titian-haired dame who is Jack Diamond's mistress in William Kennedy's *Legs*. Those are the minor characters in these dramas. Eve is not minor, of course. But walking under her image on a ceiling is much like hearing only a few spoken lines from a woman in a bit part: They share the need to make us understand instantly who they are and what they represent.

So give them red hair. Because when you do, all its associations will follow.

It has been done to people of varying rank in our moral landscape. Pity poor Cassandra, beautiful, desired, and cursed; in her the two major responses to red hair intersect. In Greek legend she is given the gift of prophecy by Apollo, who desired her because of her beauty. But when she refused him as a lover, he gave the gift a fatal twist and punished her by making everyone hearing her foretellings believe them to be lies. Of course, all of her prophecies were true. Her beauty then attracted Ajax the Lesser, who raped her during the capture of Troy, and Agamemnon, who wanted her as a sex slave but didn't listen to her wise warnings and took her home as a captive, where they were both slain by his wife, Clytemnestra. An iconographic subject for pottery, friezes, and paintings, Cassandra is one of Greek mythology's most recognizable figures, almost always portrayed with long red hair.

Consider Persephone, abducted to Hades, the underworld, becoming its queen and wife of Hades, its king. Associated with the symbols of fertility, including grain and corn, she reminds us of both Set and Typhon, though she takes on better shades of red than they do. But only to a point. After all, she spends half the year as the mate of Hades, during which time the world plunges into winter, only to rise again, as she ascends from the underworld each year on a pass to visit her mother, Demeter. When Persephone rises, mortals are delivered into spring. When I stood, awed, before her at the Ashmolean that day at Oxford after interviewing Professor Harding, Hades's wife was a red head on the canvas, as she is in countless portrayals.

When depicted by their portraitists, Eve, Mary Magdalene, Cassandra, and Persephone are represented in ways that do not require that we fully know their tales, but merely that we understand their stories through an association with one attribute: their red hair. It makes a far better identifier than a pink shirt, magenta scarf, or a blushing rose in the lapel. An essential piece of human semiotics, the iconographic wallop red hair packs is reinforced in the world's faiths, in which there are more rules about covering our hair than about anything else, except our genitalia.

My most profound experience with hair as a symbol of faith was when, in my twenties, a Hasidic woman came to call at my Manhattan apartment one afternoon to discuss a community project in which we were both involved. I had forgotten the appointment and, despite the hour, was asleep when she buzzed. I ran for the door, unlatched it, wrenched it open, and shouted for her to come upstairs, then dashed into the bathroom to dress. In seconds, even from within the bathroom, I could hear the sounds of chanting. Or mumbling.

"Rachel? Right? It's Rachel, isn't it? You in?"

The low growl continued and, when I peeked out of the bathroom, amid the clutter of my living room, was a tiny woman in a bad wig, huge topcoat, and flat shoes, talking to herself. Then I realized she was praying. I always get nervous when people pray for me, and that's what I thought—that she was praying for me—as I took in the totems of my life strewn around my apartment: perhaps five pairs of black high heels visible, unmatched, scattered about the square living room; an ashtray overflowing with butts; several evening bags on the sofa; photographs of me with various friends and boyfriends.

What I thought she saw was the mess, my choices, apparent to anyone but me that it was a life of squalid morals, teetering on the cusp of utter ruin; I was convinced that in a single second she had seen into my soul and that she was pure of heart and good, so good, in fact, that she was praying for my salvation. And whether or not she was pious, she was better than I could ever be. This train wreck of a thought had been triggered in an instant by the wig and that kryptonite word that travels with it: *modesty*. I knew enough to know that when a Jewish woman covers her hair, she does so in the name of modesty.

Modesty was not my strong suit at the time. If anything, I was brazen, staring at her. And her appearance was magnetic, nearly overpowering, especially in my small space: Her flat shoes, made of what appeared to be cardboard, primly met the hem of her plain, dour skirt, which, in turn, touched off the waistline of an oversize cardigan, buttoned all the way up; her wig; her tiny hands that fluttered when she asked for what she wanted—a glass that had never been used and soda that had never been opened.

We touched fingers when I handed her the glass, setting off another round of mumbling prayer. And it irritated me. I was nobody's foil. If I wanted a mirror to my soul, I figured, I'd use the one at Bergdorf's. I stared at her head.

"I just got married," she said, her little fingers fluttering over her head, tiny under this Darnel nest of matte brown. "So, the wig." She had married a man with three kids, in Queens, and while all of this was new to her, none of it was unwelcome, she explained. In fact, she wasn't born Jewish. She had been a Lutheran.

I flashed back to the hard wood seats and bad food of my family's Lutheran church.

"That would do it," I said.

"It did for me." And she smiled.

That kind of broke the proverbial ice. We moved slowly to the topic that had brought us together, and before the sun started to go down, we had made a date to get together again—she wanted to come back, she'd had fun, and so had I, enough, in fact, that I had settled into simple human curiosity. So I asked.

"Do you shave your head?"

"No," she said, laughing. "My husband would haaaaate that." And she lifted the wig just a little and gave the cutest little pixie cut underneath a shake that changed her, utterly and instantly, into a sorority girl. On: Religious, devout, fearsome in very bad wig of one color that made me panic in a mean-snake kind of way. Off: a woman who wanted her husband to desire her. On. Off. She smiled and dropped it back on. That is the power of hair.

* * *

The Jewish laws of modesty are intended to encourage the notion that physical beauty and love have lasting meaning rather than merely being stimuli for brief, ecstatic desire. Lack of modesty is believed to lead to the destruction of the family, and it falls to the married woman to be fastidious about her modesty, guarding her beauty for her husband. In Hebrew, the word for *bride* is *kalah*, its etymology associated with the phrase "to cover." In ancient ceremonies the bride arrived veiled, was unveiled for the ceremony, and then was covered again, never more to be viewed by the eyes of another man. Consummating the Jewish wedding service are the words "You are sanctified to me by the laws of Moshe and the Jewish People." These are stated by the groom and apparently give the wife over to the husband to be his, exclusively. To remain his requires modesty and fidelity on the part of the wife. These are among the foundations of the traditional Jewish home.

And so Rachel covered her hair, as have many Jewish women since biblical days. She was wearing a *sheitel*, Yiddish for the wig worn by married Orthodox Jewish women who wish to follow the ancient rabbinical precept forbidding women to uncover their hair in front of any men other than their husband. In the Talmud, a woman suspected of adultery is subject to the public loosening of her hair covering; the act of uncovering her hair, then, being a disgrace. An extension of this ethic was emblazoned in the public consciousness during the liberation of France in 1944, when any women accused of fraternizing with the Germans were subject to being forcibly shaved and paraded through the streets.

The covering of hair is not limited to the Jews, of course. Roman Catholic nuns, married only to Christ, traditionally wear a coif to cover theirs. And for women who are not nuns, the Bible instructs in 1 Corinthians, chapter 11, that "the head of every man is Christ" but that "the head of the woman is the man," and that men should pray with their heads uncovered but that women should pray with their heads covered or shaven, the logic being that "the woman is the glory of the man." This gave rise to the tradition still followed by many women in devout Catholic homes of covering their heads when they attend mass.

For Muslim women, it is the *khimar* that covers their head, as instructed in the Qur'an, along with other directives that instruct them to lower their gaze, guard their private parts, and not display their beauty beyond their face and hands to anyone other than those on a circumscribed list of intimates.

Are these belief systems deepened by visual cues or merely reinforced by them? And is something enforced just the same in the absence of the image? When you cover hair does it make it as highly charged as when, say, you paint it red?

The story of Eve is supposed to make us behave, reminding us that at the root of all evil is a woman whose behavior brings us the very deaths we all have to look forward to. And when Michelangelo painted the root of that evil, instead of making her ashen and invisible, worthy of no notice at all, he chose the opposite route, gifting her with the reddest mark, the original scarlet letter, the color of Cain and sanguine humor, the very color of orgasm and fire and hell. And in the presence of that, there is an absence of something else. In the same way red hair glares off the white of the skin with which it travels, the meaning of the color red opposes the meaning of covering our hair. Absent in red is any hint of modesty. And the absence of modesty is not immodesty. It is exhibitionism, with all of its fanfare ostentation. It is the desire to be seen, to be looked at, to be noticed.

With the colorization, Michelangelo ages Eve, almost disfigures her, morphing her from the most beautiful of creatures into, a mere few feet away, a near hag who struggles under the weight of the shame of her sin, under a shroud of long red hair. The artist seems to be reminding us that as it was with the mark of Cain, when cowed by God, redheads are hard to conceal.

Which is just the way some men like it. Flamboyant, attracting our attention, flame-colored women are easy to spot and hard to miss, and in art, make marvelous icons for our passionate wants. And just as the kiss of Judas versus that of Lilith illustrates the divide between how we feel about red-haired men and their female counterparts, it is again to the head of Lilith we must return when looking for the original redheaded icon of sexual desire. When it comes to painting Lilith, the undisputed master was Dante Gabriel Rossetti.

Rossetti was part of a movement whose seriousness of purpose is well expressed in its name, the Pre-Raphaelite Brotherhood. Pledged to restore art to an ethic before that of Raphael—whose ability they did not fault, but whose methods of having assistants mass produce the artist's ideas they abhorred—they did not mass produce their ideals. While we refer to them as a group, each artist had his own periods of diverse work: In the 1850s Rossetti was awash in medieval-ized watercolors; by the mid-1860s he had returned to oils, a medium far more appropriate for the densely sexual, opulent, long look he then chose to have at female beauty.

The artists called the women who modeled for them, "stunners," and to refer to Rossetti's resulting pictures as "portraits" suggests middling anemia, like an inability to discern skim milk from cream, a dinner date from erotic hunger. And while not all of them were redheads—the queen of the stunners, Jane Morris, had dark brown hair—there were three red-haired women whose lives will always be inextricably linked with Rossetti: Elizabeth Siddall, Fanny Cornforth, and Alexa Wilding. He married the first, kept Fanny as a mistress, and chose the third to illustrate the ultimate changeling.

In 1865 Alexa Wilding was walking down a London street when Rossetti fell in step next to her, taken by her auburn hair. They agreed that she would come the next day to his art studio. She stood him up. Weeks later he saw her again on the Strand and this time she came, then went on to become the model who sat for more of his finished paintings than any other.

According to Rossetti's assistant, Alexa Wilding's was "the very type of face he had been seeking so long," framed by a purling mass of "golden, auburn hair." And she could go both ways. She would become the personification of poetic beauty, the model of Sibylla Palmifera, the image of a soul's loveliness for whom Rossetti would write an accompanying sonnet, in which she would be referred to as "beauty enthroned." And she would be the model for its evil twin. Because the painting that Rossetti chose to accompany it was one of Lilith, the most dangerous woman who ever lived and who, for some, is the true first woman, that first object of desire, the one who bucked, Eve's illustrious predecessor, Adam's first wife. Fleeing Adam, she became a succubus—a word whose earliest use defines a female demon who has intercourse with men in their sleep, but whose etymology evolved to become synonymous with a strumpet or prostitute.

Imagine sitting down to paint a succubus, the personification of evil, to render the portrait of a woman bold enough to offer temptation to the devil himself. Part of her allure would have to be her beauty, since Lilith's tale is associated with desire, and, besides, painting an unattractive depiction of her would defeat the purpose of enticing the viewer toward the frame. Of course, art does not always follow the lines of logic; no lesser artist than Leonardo da Vinci created many wildly popular studies of the grotesque aspects of human variation. So we must consult what references were available to Rossetti upon which to draw his image of Lilith.

Reviewing existing source material on Lilith, Rossetti would have found much on her looks, her otherworldly qualities as well as her lustrous hair, all identifiers as old as her story itself. He would have discovered that when the Christians inherited the tradition of Lilith they colorized her amazing trademark, her hair, to golden red.

Being a poet as well as a painter, Rossetti added a voice to Lilith in his 1869 poem "Eden Bower." There, Lilith speaks directly to Satan, offering her magnificent self—"How shall we mingle our love's caresses, I in thou coils and thou in my tresses!"—braiding their striking qualities of his slithering and her hair into one. And when Rossetti painted that hair, the very place Lilith offers to the devil for their mingling, he does so in an astonishing shade of red.

The poem is on view with the painting, inscribed in the huge gold frame, as the centerpiece of the astonishing Bancroft collection, currently housed at the Delaware Museum of Art, in Wilmington.

Of Adam's first wife, Lilith, it is told
(The witch he loved before the gift of Eve)
That, ere the snake's, her sweet tongue could deceive,
And her enchanter hair was the first gold.

As I read it, Margaretta Frederick, the collection's curator, interrupted me.

"That line from shoulder to throat, it's impossible, of course," she said, pointing out, as nearly everyone does, the technical mishaps of Rossetti. And she's right. What is exposed is a too vast expanse of the white flesh, anatomically incorrect but also as erotically exact as a snow-white peach and its crimson core. Its message is the opposite of modesty. Its mistress couldn't care less what you think; absorbed in her hand mirror, Lady Lilith notices the onlooker not at all. She is the poster girl for erotic self-absorption, for an utter lack of modesty, moving from carnal to character to caricature in one single canvas. Large and lush, she is desire, lust, beauty, and sin, as well as the image of conceited contentment.

The poem later concludes that after her spell goes through a man, she leaves "his straight neck bent / And round his heart one strangling golden hair," golden being interchangeable with red in many references. Lilith's hair imagery always makes her easy to find, remaining like those after-bubbles you get floating in your line of vision following a flash picture. And for good reason. She is painted/sculpted/frescoed/carved with a history of who she is, the very thing that scares us most: our own desire.

Mirroring the themes portrayed on Michelangelo's Sistine Chapel ceiling, Lilith appears in Rossetti's poem associated with the serpent who gets between Adam and Eve.

On the Sistine Chapel ceiling, Lilith, in serpent form, has encased herself in the ultimate phallic imagery, planning to tempt not Adam, but Eve, bone of his bone, and bring about the Fall of man. Having had her turn with Adam, she had been replaced and now tempts Eve with the fruit of the tree of knowledge. Eve is said in Genesis to recognize that the tree of knowledge was "good for food," "a delight to the eyes," as well as able to "make one wise." But it was also forbidden. Genesis tells us that the words coming from the snake were reassuring, promising, "Your eyes shall be opened."

When the serpent is depicted as a woman tempting another woman, it flies in the face of our traditional images of Satan as a male but not that of allurement being the realm of women. Doubly female in its imagery, the rendition of serpent-as-woman-tempting-woman makes the hellish point that women are the conduits through which and into which original sin was passed. Physiognomics and sympathetic magic allow us to redden anyone who hooks up with Satan. From Satan to Lilith, from Lilith to Eve, the color of evil appears to have sympathetically passed, so that on Eve, the red marks her with our ultimately unsettling theme: desire.

Though few of us in contemporary society think that desire is necessarily evil, it is impossible to ignore its strong associations to sin: We are supposed to have sex to continue the race, but our traditions are unclear as to just how much we are supposed to enjoy it. Women need not enjoy it at all in order to fulfill the biological destiny of procreation. But do they? Perhaps the greatest value of the color red may be right here, in its ability to illustrate our ultimate tremulous spot—the fine line of that changeling moment when the giver of pleasure becomes the taker of pleasure, as well. Through superstition, myth, and religion, we have been carefully taught what happens when those first women succumbed to their desires. And you can capture this ideal—if you use the red on your palette.

CHAPTER SEVEN

You May Be Many Things, Young Lady, but You Are No Redhead

The Tangle of Sex and Science Are but Two Strands of the Braid

T HE FOLLOWING experiment is not for the faint of heart.

1. Find yourself a big redhead.
2. Take her to Harry Winston.

But call first. Tell them you are bringing in a redhead to fit a necklace on her lovely white throat and some earrings for those seashell ears of hers. They'll ready a selection for you.

And when you get there, the well-manicured salesperson will have prepared a tray of emeralds, and you won't be the least bit surprised. But watch the redhead's eyes. They will dart toward the rubies.

Why emeralds? Because across the color chart from red is green. Painters know that to shade red, you don't add black; you add green. Green tempers red, tones it, makes it less vibrant, more earthy. And green is what people have been offering to redheads for years in clothing, jewelry, and even eye shadow. Everyone thinks we should look divine in green and we do. But red is our color, our perfect backdrop, accessory, and highlight.

Why rubies? To a redhead, the better way to shade our color is to deepen it by adding more red.

There has always been a disconnect between the way redheads are seen and how we see ourselves. The world wants us in green, but we prefer red. As a child whose mother and grandmother (neither of them redheads) chose my clothes, I was always told never to wear red, that it clashed with my hair. As an adult, my closet is full of it. And that's not surprising since color is wildly subjective. We see what we want, we see what we are trained to see, and we miss the rest. The Heisenberg uncertainty principle reminds us of the risk of observing anything, understanding that when you shine light on something, all you may in fact be recording is a reflection of your own illumination. That kind of reverse observation emerges when we think of redheads. Pick a redhead, any redhead. What do you see?

Take, for example, Prince Harry. Chances are excellent that he has great knowledge of his royal lineage, that he, more than many of us, knows who he is. And yet Buckingham Palace has been forced to foil plots to steal a lock of his hair in order to challenge his paternity. The *Sunday Times* reported that one such heist aimed to get a sample of his DNA. The younger son of Prince Charles and the late Princess Diana, Prince Harry is particularly notable for his shock of red hair. The color, some people think, might have come through his mother's admitted infidelity with a former British Army officer, James Hewitt, although that adulterous paternity has been denied on all sides. It is inevitable that the DNA will be examined at some point, but even if the science of genetics confirms Harry's lineage in the House of Windsor, I will put serious money against anyone who thinks that will change the mind of a single person who is convinced Harry is the love child of the princess and the playboy.

That would be asking too much of science. It can't cool all of our hot-tempered responses to things, allay every one of our foolish fears, or demystify the myriad enticements in some people's allure. It would be nice if it made us reasonable enough to allow Harry's hair, at the very least, a bit of privacy. But it won't. Because humans are passionate—something that is biological in its base but mythic in its story.

I know this from my own pursuit of this topic. Having traveled extensively, given blood, looked at cages of mice, sifted through ancient texts, viewed paintings and mosaics, and interviewed scientists, all in an effort to identify red hair, I have tried to remain neutral in my conclusions, but it has proved impossible. Some of what I've observed is almost magnetic in its draw; certain identifiers have real appeal. Not all. A little of this, a little of that—I have consciously added ingredients of both science and sex to the recipe of my own identity.

For instance, my sense of being a redhead is now more focused on and by images of power. This ideal is readily personified in the strength of several iconic redheads. Boudicca, queen of the Icenis, for example: Ruthless as the Romans made her out to be, she is a great role model for anyone with a British heritage, for all women, but for redheads in particular, and for me, specifically. So I have tucked the association into my persona to pull out during my own, admittedly lesser, battles. Some redheads have rubbed off in ways that make me feel stronger by association. Even among the images of evil that I've perused, there have been a few takeaways; I find the idea of being a little bit bad—as well as enticing someone else to be so—undeniably alluring, perhaps even promising.

Nearing the end of this project, looking around my office, I find that I have surrounded myself with images of redheads. Many are reproductions of the faces of Dante Gabriel Rossetti's "stunners." But other artists and other images are represented, as well. *Eve Overcome by Remorse*, by Anna Lea Merritt (1844–1930), portrays a redhead slumped over a bitten apple. Merritt's *Lamia, the Serpent Woman* shows her slithering up a tree while exposing her white breasts beneath her very red hair. Lamia, another name for Lilith, is everywhere in my office, perhaps my favorite being her depiction by the Honorable John Collier (1850–1934) as a standing, naked, red-haired woman whose face reveals the ecstasy aroused in her by the thick serpent coiling up her ample body.

A postcard reproduction of *The Kelpie* by Herbert James Draper (1864–1920) is part of a small shrine on my desk. A Scottish water spirit, the kelpie has a changeling aspect of both evil and good and is reputed to either cause drownings or to warn those in danger of drowning. Red-haired, in the small reproduction, and gloriously naked, she idly observes a stream from a languid pose on a rock. In my office she keeps vigil over one of my inheritances from my Victorian grandfather—the glass slide, now stored in a Tupperware container. Years ago, someone shoved the slide into its cheap frame and mistakenly inserted a white backing, making it impossible to discern anything more than a ghostly outline of a man. Despite its shadowy nature, I believe the slide is of Alexander Johnston, my great-great-grandfather, the rigger, and that the kelpie should do penance for his drowning in the Mersey River.

Also adorning my workspace are pictures of the Red Heads, a 1930s women's basketball team. Their uniform hair color, initially supplied at the beauty shops around Cassville, Missouri, first made them the talk of the town and then, as the All-American Red Heads, the talk of the country as they became a much sought-after exhibition team, like the Harlem Globetrotters.

In terms of blatant commercial sex appeal, my roccellin favorite is an Aussie icon of brilliant typecast marketing. Miss Redhead is the logo for an Australian match company founded in 1909, whose earliest products were the red-tipped, "strike anywhere" version that are particularly sensitive to friction, and are well personified by a foxy, red-haired mascot. Somebody sent me a box of the matches and I love it, particularly placed on my windowsill alongside a miniature Anne of Green Gables doll, her red hair a flaming reminder of her personality.

These collected representatives of redheads contain aspects of identity that I'd like to possess. For instance, having previously bought into the myth that redheads are emotionally explosive, I realize that I've let myself off easy too many times with the misguided reassurance that it was simply my nature to be combative. Instead, using the dual meaning of the kelpie as my guide, I might allow those surges of high emotion to alert me to the danger ahead if I encourage the worst to unfold. Given the chance, any redhead can select to fill in or edit out existing stereotypes, puttying in her rougher spots with warmer shades, and heightening with aspects needed for strength. Without this, we are left to what we were told, the things we are taught by others about ourselves.

Research about hair uncovers a lot of relics. Particularly important in Roman Catholic and Orthodox churches, relics can be part of a body or some personal memorial of a martyr, saint, or other sacred person that is preserved for veneration. In its turn, veneration adds a spicy ingredient to the identity of the relic: its etymology reveals a strong connection to soliciting the goodwill of an ancient god, specifically Venus, goddess of love and beauty, whose name comes from the Latin stem of a neutral common noun meaning "physical desire, sexual appetite."

Desiring something from our saints, martyrs, and sacred persons, we make pilgrimages. The relics of Mary Magdalene, for instance, are said to be housed in a great cathedral in France, an edifice built around the discovery of her remains. A bit of what is said to be her skin is on view there in a crystal tube. It didn't tempt me, though, having come long ago to a strong suspicion of ordained items, preferring to think that relics, like desire, are subjective and deeply individualized in their draw.

The idea of a different kind of pilgrimage was tempting, however. Choosing to pay a devotional visit to a redhead whose life and work had inspired mine, I went to Amherst. It was to view a lock of hair from a woman who once described herself as "small like the wren; and my hair is bold, like the Chestnut Bur; and my eyes, like sherry in the glass, that the guest leaves."

A fan, I had been to Emily Dickinson's house before,

perhaps a dozen times, the loveliest visit being on my honeymoon, walking the path between the Homestead, where she had lived, and the Evergreens, the next-door house of Austin, her brother, and his family. "A path between, just wide enough for two who love," according to the poet. I took my husband there to walk it with me and recited that line for him. But in those previous visits I had never viewed Emily Dickinson's hair.

Emily Dickinson and Thomas Wentworth Higginson, an editor at the *Atlantic Monthly*, corresponded for more than twenty years. In July 1862, he requested a picture of her. She demurred, describing herself instead, in the quote above about the wren and the wine.

But in 1853, Emily Dickinson had cut off a lock of her hair, folded it into a tiny paper parcel, and sent it off to her friend Emily Fowler Ford, who kept it. Recently viewing a photograph of it, I found the lock to be the most curious hair in captivity, a relic. In the picture, the hair looked red.

The pilgrimage requires visiting the Archives and Special Collections Department at Amherst College's Robert Frost Library. Prior correspondence deemed that I had legitimate reason for viewing it and, having made an appointment to do so, I am told to carry nothing into the room. Signing waivers with the archive's pens, and then keeping my hands on the table, as instructed—no touching is allowed—I wait for the lock of hair to be brought out and placed on the table. Then, the paper package holding the relic is slowly unfolded by Daria D'Arienzo, head of Archives and Special Collections.

Inside the origami-like packet is the lock, curled like a dormant fox. The hair is a vibrant red. On the paper in which it is lain is a hue very unlike that of sherry in a glass; it is rather, the boldest impression of claret, which seems to have seeped into the paper.

In Dublin, I had visited Trinity College Library to see the Book of Kells, an ancient Latin tome of the four Gospels of the New Testament. Known as an illuminated manuscript, it is handwritten and decorated in brilliant colors; "illumination" originally denoted a text embellished with gold or silver but later was taken to mean early manuscripts in general. The Book of Kells is breathtaking in its colors, particularly its red, and gazing at Emily's hair, I thought of the book's ancient paint: the gold procured from the precious metal, the blues sent from distant mines of lapis lazuli. To come close to matching the lock of hair, we'd need to grind rubies with amber.

Seeing my delight as I peer into the lock, Ms. D'Arienzo says, "Well, we almost never bring this out, but have a look." Suddenly, there under my eyes is the daguerreotype. The original, in its small frame. You know the image it contains: the poet sits demurely, her hair parted in the middle, a ribbon on her neck. Taken in 1847, when Emily Dickinson was sixteen, it is the sole incontrovertible likeness of her. And looking at it, I am also able to see the gap between the woman I had always thought she was in the daguerreotype versus what that lock of ravishing red hair does to colorize her identity. The color changes everything.

Why?

Because I had always thought Emily Dickinson was plain. We're taught it in school, we see it in the picture, and we apply the idea as background to the work. Her plainness is defined as an integral part of the poet's identity, wrongly used to explain her reclusive nature. In today's terms, the poet probably suffered from a social phobia. It is too simple to say that being plain, she stayed in. But until this moment, I had believed she was plain.

No redheads, though, are plain. You might not find all redheads attractive; I have heard people insist that they find no redhead attractive, citing our light-colored eyelashes and diaphanous eyebrows that wash out our features. In the 2004 novel *Jonathan Strange and Mr Norrell*, by Susanna Clarke, the narrator emphatically declares about the magician Jonathan Strange that "his hair had a reddish tinge and, as everybody knows, no one with red hair can ever truly be said to be handsome." Later in the book, the character of Mr. Norrell, also a magician, refers to the trait of Jonathan Strange by declaring, "Reddish-brown is such a fickle colour." Some people dislike freckles, preferring unmarked skin; others are badly shocked by the vividness of our axillary hair. There are those who think that the character traits that travel with the hair color render us unattractive. But any idea of plainness is simply contrary to the fancy color that is red.

Seeing my response to the lock alongside the daguerreotype, Ms. D'Arienzo suggests that I contact a certain Emily Dickinson scholar to learn more about the poet's hair color. I had previously read this scholar's work, so I shot off an e-mail to her upon my return home. Within minutes came the following reply:

> *To Marion Roach*
>
> *In response to your inquiry—I do not consider Emily Dickinson as a person with "red hair," though there are those who would disagree with me. My impression is that when she was young her hair had a reddish cast. Martha Dickinson Bianchi, her niece, remembered her as an*

*adult with hair "of that same warm bronze chestnut hue
that Titian immortalized."*

Amazed, I e-mailed right back, asking, "But have you
seen it?"

"Yes," she replied.

The "but" in my argument held no sway with the scholar.
Emily Dickinson was not a person with red hair because the
color did not appear red to that observer. A simple declaration of empirical observation, it reminded me of Dr. Rees's
trouble in classifying redheads: one writer's vermilion is
another's "reddish cast." To me, the identity of Emily
Dickinson was enhanced when she was revealed to be a
redhead, informing me that when she wrote in the poem
that begins "Wild Nights—Wild Nights! Were I with thee,"
that my high school suspicion—which, at the time, was
slavishly refuted by my prim, girls' school English teacher—
was true. I didn't suspect then that Emily was writing to
God and I sure as hell don't think so now.

The subjectivity of the contemporary Dickinson scholar
amazed me. To me, Emily's hair was red and yet someone
who had devoted her professional life's work to the poet
would not consider it so. Wondering about the scholar's
position on the hair color, I concluded that there must be
certain people in the world who would prefer that certain
other people were not red-haired; that it might be inap-
propriate for certain people to be so.

There is schadenfreude, of course, that old satisfaction or
pleasure we take at someone else's misfortune. This feeling
also provokes resentment from anyone who glories in anything that she has not earned. In that vein, some people
disdain bottle redheads, apparently thinking one of two

things: that the woman who has chosen the color simply looks unattractive in it or that she can't live up to the reputation of the redhead.

This failure at being a true-to-type redhead is even possible in the world of dolls. It happened to Midge. You know Barbie, of course. And if you do, you've probably seen Midge, a freckle-faced redhead who popped out of the box in 1963. Recently, Midge got pregnant (Baby Doctor Barbie was scheduled to do the delivery). I was not at all surprised that when the doll makers chose one icon on which to market test a pregnancy, they chose Midge, the redhead. It seemed absolutely logical that the red-haired friend would be the one to get pregnant.

It also didn't surprise me that when pregnant Midge showed up in 2002 on the shelves of a Wal-Mart in Yorktown, Virginia, the *Hampton Roads Daily Press* reported that she was unshelved and placed under the counter. Swifter than you can say positive Wasserman test. After that, if you wanted to purchase pregnant Midge, you had to ask.

While the public's negative response was surely due more to the pregnancy than the hair color, it offers a lovely lesson. After all, the company didn't try to market a knocked-up Barbie. Instead, they impregnated Midge, perhaps concluding that a pregnant redhead might fly under the radar of moral outrage. But the marketers undervalued that supremely sacred state: pregnancy.

Not only are there some persons who should not be persons with red hair, but there are some things that even a redhead cannot get away with.

In my early thirties, I was in a whirlwind romance with someone who, right after we met, came away with me for a while before introducing me to his family. And when we returned to New York, at a dinner when I finally met his parents, the son made some proud reference to my red hair, to which the father angrily spat out, "You may be many things, young lady, but you are no redhead." I never figured out if he didn't like me because I was quite apparently a redhead or if he thought that my behavior with his son somehow took away my status as one, or if it was simply the first stupid nasty thing that came to his mind. I didn't stick around long enough to find out. Under the circumstances, I would have been less shocked if he had said, "You may be many things, you redhead, but you are no lady." There, he might have had me.

But denying my hair color was shocking to me. Adolescent in its foulness as well as utterly without basis—at the time I had very long, very red hair—his response felt like a punch in the jaw. That he didn't like me was okay, but his denying who I am was not. This is because I define myself in part by my color. And I know it is the proverbial slippery slope: That there are associations with red hair I utterly reject and others I wear proudly means nothing to anyone else, since I don't get to choose how the observer sorts those same traits. Grazing through the stereotypes, I am on the delicatessen plan, winding a way over the menu offerings, picking, choosing and rejecting; adhering to some, dismissing others. Having adopted a method of personal vigilance that allows me to be on the lookout for associations that suffuse my color with preferred associations and to reject those I choose not to adopt, I enhance my self-image. But to other people my red hair is more a take-it-or-leave-it experience: Red-haired, to them, I may also be a certain type of person, complete with temperament.

As if to illustrate this divide, a story arrived over the e-mail transom from Pablo Fenjves, a redheaded Argentine screenwriter in Los Angeles.

> *A young Jewish man excitedly tells his mother he's fallen in love and is going to get married. He says, "Just for fun, Ma, I'm going to bring over three women and you try and guess which one I'm going to marry." The mother agrees. The next day he brings three beautiful women into the house and sits them down on the couch and they chat for a while. He then says, "Okay, Ma. Guess which one I'm going to marry." She immediately replies, "The redhead in the middle."*
>
> *"That's amazing, Ma. You're right. How did you know?"*
>
> *"I don't like her."*

Happily, science is engaged in far more serious debates as to whether or not redheads are likable.

The British press recently reported that the MC1R would be used to identify the hair color of a killer, via a DNA diagnosis of exclusion: based on blood spatter left at the scene, the lab would, at the very least, know whether the killer was a redhead. The hope is that soon forensic scientists will be able to tell the race and physical features of a criminal as well, what one story dubbed a "genetic photo-fit."

It is an important advance in solving crime and a welcome addition to the toolbox of the forensic sciences. It may become another science-based diagnostic piece of distinguishing equipment—like fingerprints—and replace the more fallible witness-based identification system that has put thousands of innocent people in prison, including many on death row. But the advance is also bound to raise hell if, instead of identifying hair color by the blood left behind, this science is applied to skin color.

Redheads are not a race, of course. But they do provide a less-loaded place to cast our eyes when considering color. Mostly white, redheads are nearly all Caucasian. But after Jonathan Rees's identification of the gene, not only is it possible to see redheads as genetically distinguished within the Caucasian race, but it has also become possible for scientists to advance ideas on personalized medicine.

A breakthrough 2002 study linked a visible genetic trait to doses of anesthesia. The first link was made from a University of Louisville study that reported naturally red-headed women require 20 percent more anesthesia than anyone else. Dr. Daniel Sessler, the study's author, warned that inadequate doses of anesthesia could allow people to wake up during surgery or to have increased recall of the procedure, an experience that some redheads have reported.

An Associated Press story included a comment from Dr. Andrea Kurz of Washington University in St. Louis: "Anesthesiologists have long grumbled that redheads can be a little harder to put under, but no one ever studied if that was real or folklore."

I could have told them it was real. On several occasions, when having in-office procedures for which anesthesia was administered, I remained fully awake. Once, to the utter amazement of a Manhattan doctor, I read a book through an entire procedure. At the time, the physician said he had never seen anything like it; he shook his head and noted it on my record. After that, I continued to tell doctors of my difficulty in going under; they continued to undermedicate me, and I read a lot of books during various procedures.

In 2003, the Louisville study was advanced by another study published in the *Proceedings of the National Academy of Sciences*. The lead researcher, Jeffery Mogil, a McGill University professor of psychology, reported that he and his colleagues had identified the candidate gene that may be responsible. It is, of course, the MC1R, variants of which cause red hair and pale skin.

It seems that in both the Louisville and the McGill studies, anecdotal history about red hair provided scientists with something positive to prove—that story preceded fact and that the resulting relationship is very beneficial indeed.

When peering into the eugenics hair-color files, I had seen only the pernicious end of the anecdote/science relationship. Now, I was reading about a purely positive outcome from such a pairing and wondered what other, unstudied cousins of this collusion of story and science existed in popular culture. A real inventory of what we simply believe about red hair as well as what we believe *in*—some measure of our contemporary mix of fact and fiction—seemed appropriate. And so I went to a sperm bank.

The Web site of the California Cryobank invites men to donate sperm after filling out a Keirsey Temperament Sorter and "self reporting" about how many years of college they attended, what they do, what they like, and, in short, who they think they are: seventy zippy questions taking less than fifteen minutes to answer. (This begs a moment of scrutiny, of course, on the quantum relationship between numbers of the truths historically told prior to the promise of ejaculation. But I stray.)

The Keirsey whacks us all into one of the four temperaments, or four basic people patterns—artisan, guardian, idealist, rational—each of which can be further divided into four, resulting in sixteen variants. Interestingly, there is that association with the four again, like the humors and the elements. The Keirsey is not alone in its four-ness when allocating personality type: The most widely used personality indicator, the Myers-Briggs Type Indicator, focuses on four polarities, taking its cues from Carl Gustav Jung, the early-twentieth-century Swiss psychologist who put us all up into four basic types, as did his contemporary, Rudolf Steiner, who lectured about four temperaments: choleric, sanguine, phlegmatic, and melancholic.

Looking at the Keirsey in purely selective terms, the woman wanting to reproduce can select for a specific look—red hair being one of the categories—and then within that color, select for temperament. The fact that temperament flows from color in this selection process suggests that popular culture accepts that some patterns of human behavior are inherited along color lines. It could sound oh so eugenic. And uninformed. And reasonable. It seems that not all that deep down in our beliefs remains this idea of a pairing between our color and our character. What's more, apparently, even at our most biologically clinical—when reproducing via Federal Express—we defer to these beliefs when choosing a mate. Market driven, the sperm bank wouldn't package the product this way if the public wasn't buying it.

Science, too, is doing good business when it looks at my color. The mere discovery of the need for anesthesia is proof enough for me: While to some I appear rambunctious, perhaps even inexhaustible (a true characterization of me that happens to be supported by myth and history—think

Boudicca), it is also clinically proven that I am hard to knock out (now a scientific fact). But my prediction is that the ideas we carry and the things we learn will not cancel out one another. Red hair will never shed its sexy skin even when the most virulent of redhead myths are tempered by the realities of the science of hair color; one will not permanently supersede the other. They are twins that will wrestle all our lives.

It is the longer, less personal view that makes this clear. Looking back four hundred years ago, for instance, when it was believed to be poisonous, the fat of a red-haired man was a needed ingredient in a deadly concoction. These days, a drop of blood from a red-haired woman reveals why she is hard to sedate. Related ideas, both beliefs were preceded by stories that led to inquiry. Inquiry, in turn, led to application, albeit deadly in the case of the poison. In fact, it is toxic to consume human matter: drinking human blood will make a person deathly ill. It just doesn't need to be the blood of a red-haired man—or the remains of his rendered fat. The by-products of redheads probably did kill some people. What lived on was the recipe as well as the tale, until one was proved immoral and the other became a mere curiosity that outraged me when I first read it. Story to inquiry to truth to story to inquiry. On it goes, but not without evoking passionate response. Because on the subject of our color, no one is impartial.

For my part, I know that I am less neutral than ever on the topic of red hair.

When Dr. Rees had questioned the very color of my hair—"is it dyed?"—a sore point was struck that simply did not surrender to reason. The truth is, I've started to fade. In the past few years I've twice had people describe my hair as "brown," and both times I've corrected them, only to notice something in their eyes that pretty much registered, "Yeah, whatever," like it didn't matter. It did to me.

Something changed for me after I saw Rees in Edinburgh. More than anything I wanted my genetic credentials for my red hair, whether heterozygous and having two different alleles, or homozygous and having two alleles that are the same for the changes that produce my color. Thinking about the impending results of the blood drawn in Edinburgh, I realized that I had begun to consider my gene sequencing as a kind of legitimizing status, proof that I am a redhead in full. Instead of holding to my own theory that the science and the story are equal as well as equalizing, I had let the science plunge ahead in some kind of race I was running in my head. So much so, that when arriving at my next destination I simply couldn't justify having traveled there.

After leaving Rees's lab, I am booked for three days in Southport, England, where my English grandfather met Margaret Pilkington, my English redheaded grandmother. And within minutes of arriving, I can't imagine what I'm doing here.

Making things worse is the fact that the British genealogist I had hired before leaving home has yet to turn up anything. As I had moved from London to Oxford, and then on to Edinburgh, I had checked in daily, hoping for something to relate a hair color going further back than the relatives I had known—perhaps to my Danish great-great-grandfather, the rigger. His name was all I had, and with no existing data on the man, the inquiry was stuck right there.

Checking into the hotel in Southport, I receive a curt e-mail update from the genealogist, who was pursuing my instruction to turn his sights on this town. He has found only this: Margaret Pilkington (my red-haired grand-mother), "*born April 14, 1881, Ormskirk; Louisa Pilking-ton, born 1887, Ormskirk, as well. Father, John P., asphelter, mother Margaret Twist married 1877, Ormskirk, Both Margaret and John alive in the 1881 census, other children: James, 3 Mary Jane, 1. One address, in Birkdale.*" Nothing about my grandfather's side of this family. And no burial records.

You go with what you've got. Down to the concierge, where a review of local maps reveals that the address in Birkdale has been swallowed up; the road no longer exists. Outside to check with a cabbie to be sure. Never heard of it.

Damn it.

Not a building, school, or church whose records I might view, no homes to look at, no one to see. I have come all this way and booked this room for three nights for no good reason. Back upstairs in my room, I imagine myself merely walking the streets where my grandparents met and courted; there is nothing more to be learned from that than what I can see from this window: this Victorian seaside town of gooseneck streetlamps and its peaked roofs, closer to God and the rain.

Instead, sitting down with my laptop, I begin to make notes about sequencing my gene as simply a contemporary cousin of what people do when tracking back their origi-nating heritage. When they define themselves as French American, Chinese American, African American, we cer-tainly understand. It's a matter of definition, reaching back into the genetic etymology to clarify our meaning. I find myself typing: "DNA reveals not only our racial identity but our personal identity, as well. I want that. I can't have a truly personal identity without my genetic story."

Which is odd, since to this point in life I have had no interest in my genealogy. The first time I realized that each of my grandparents had four grandparents of their own and that those four each had another four, the sheer numbers had created a numbing sensation I embraced as boredom.

I'm not alone, though in biological terms it sometimes feels that way, having only one living blood relative, my sister, Margaret. We are very dissimilar, having grown up more like curios each had inherited than relatives one resembled. Our differences are as basic as our looks, the latter living examples of Mendel's law of segregation. She is what was genetically selected from our mother's side, a brunette with the small intensity of a pencil drawing; I am a tall redhead whose countenance might best be represented in a child's finger painting. Among the things we did share, however, was an utter lack of interest in our roots.

Perhaps this is compounded by the fact that neither of us has biological children. My daughter is adopted from China, a marvel which has thrown open a whole new continent for our exploration, but hardly beckons us backward into my ancestry. And as I am thinking this, I realize that purely in terms of red hair, I am the end of a line, one that perhaps travels back to the very first redhead. Since it can't go forward, the obvious next best thing is to go in reverse. But the genealogist is stuck.

I dial the Lancashire Records Office. I'll go there and look for myself. But first I need directions.

The clerk who answers the phone is named John Benson. He advises against a visit: the office has moved way out of town, he says, much farther than I thought from my hotel. I should try the crematorium, he recommends. Everyone, it seems, passes through the Lancashire crematorium one way or the other.

I call there only to find that Sandra in the crematorium records office has nothing.

I call back John Benson again, and this time I must sound like I'm about to cry.

"What are you looking for?" he asks me.

"What do I want, you mean?" I badger the kind man. "One of my own."

"Hold on." And this time I do—for fifteen minutes as I watch the clock—thinking about what I had just admitted, wondering what John Benson must think of me.

There was no hello again, there was simply this: "Where are you right now?"

"The Prince of Wales Hotel."

"Oh, that's good. If you go out the front door and make a left, then make another left, and walk down that street." Minutes later, I am standing with Neville Green, the warden on duty by the entry booth of the Duke Street cemetery, a map laid out before us. We are running our hands over the paper in the light rain, trying to locate Section H, number 2700. Neville looks around, nods, and says, "I've nothing to do. Take you myself."

Slowly, we begin to make our way through the Victorian-era cemetery of peaked stones and flowering cherry trees. We pass a stone dedicated to a Southport family lost on the *Titanic*. There is a gigantic, slope-sided tribute to the clan whose company sold sewing machines, the memorial an enlarged but exactly shaped stone version of the wooden case I have in my attic, the one my grandmother dragged from this very seaside town to the Merseyside docks, into her new life in Brooklyn. A hundred yards or so farther in the rain, and then Neville says gently, "There you go. Leave you here. Wait for you by the house." He nods at another row and quietly slips away.

At first I just outline the top of the stone with my fingers, lightly touching its cool peak. Then, fingering the letters of each word:

In Loving Memory of John Pilkington, of Southport,
Who died July 21st, 1888 age 35 years.
Thy Will be Done.
Also James Pilkington, son of the above,
Who died Oct. 8th 1901 aged 25 years.
Long was his sufferings and patient, in path.
Trusting in the Lord. Also of Margaret,
wife of the above John Pilkington,
who died Feb 17th, 1927, aged 72 years,
"reunited" also Jean and Louisa Pilkington.

Running my hands along their names, I start to tell them about James Pilkington Roach, the son of the man who married their sister and child, by the looks of things, the first in this line to go to college, who was the editor of his college newspaper and went on to become the sports editor of the *New York Times*, to marry, have two children; and about those girls, telling them all about my sister and her magnificent success, an editor in chief, "the Boss," as my English grandfather always called her even when she was a child. They'd be so proud of her, I say, that fierce force that she can be; about me, my husband and our wonderful child so far away. And after a while I sink down onto the grass, stroking the turf, telling them everything I can think to say of the gratitude and respect I have for their hard lives and the endeavor that was theirs, that we share.

And finally, when it was time to go, I remember that tradition of leaving something on the grave. I hadn't thought to bring anything. I never thought I'd find them; I'd dashed from the hotel. But I have my Swiss Army knife, and with it, I cut off a lock of my red hair and bury it against the stone.

An hour later, back in the hotel room, transcribing the notes onto my laptop, I see the word "Look," and I remember just when I wrote it in my notebook. It was during the bus ride out of Downe after visiting Darwin's house, just a few days before, as I laid my head against the broad bus windows and thought of how he had looked at things; Darwin was reported by his gardener to have sat in a patio chair for hours watching the bees come and go from a single bloom.

But after walking Darwin's "sandwalk," as he called it, the path he took every day, after eating lunch in his kitchen, looking at how he laid out his perennial beds, I came to think of Darwin as a great observer of the very things we can all see if we are looking. And while common sense prevents me from comparing myself to him in any way, simple humanity does not. Look, I had thought. Look. I had scratched the word in my reporter's notebook. Look. Now I am looking. I am looking down at my black sweater, where several long red hairs whorl on the front, shed from simple motion, and what I know is that inside every human hair are great secrets.

The color links me in obvious ways to my father. But inside a hair itself, regardless of color, whirl many deeper ancestral clues. Each hair on your body grows from a skin pocket known as a follicle. A root bulb connects each hair to that follicle. Plucked hairs include this root bulb which, in turn, contain cells with nuclei, which themselves contain two strands of DNA—one from each of your parents. This is called nuclear, or genomic, DNA.

In the shaft of the hair is mitochondrial DNA, genetic material that is only inherited from our mothers. All the children of the same mother will in turn have the same mitochondrial DNA. It is more abundant and more stable than nuclear DNA.

In the shaft is also a time line. Each month, the hair on the human head grows one centimeter, or almost half an inch. In 1981 it was discovered that the presence of cocaine could not only be detected in the hair but that the months of its use could be tracked, accumulating in an ordinal way along the shaft. Soon, of course, many other drugs were also shown to be apparent in the hair, among them caffeine, heroin, and Prozac.

In your hair, then, is your history. And not only your recent history of drug use. For instance, there is the tale of your own conception.

Nuclear DNA, which is present in the head of the sperm, and mitochondrial DNA, present in its tail, part company when the head of the sperm enters the egg and unites with the ovum's nucleus. At this point, the tail falls off, leaving the father's mitochondrial DNA out of the recipe.

But you can go even further back. Since mitochondrial DNA comes from your mother, it also comes from her mother and her mother, and on and on back in time, leading some people to believe that we can trace all of us back to several mothers of the world. In fact there is a business in

Oxford dedicated to just that: You send them some blood and they will tell you from which of the so-called Seven Daughters of Eve you descend, because mitochondrial DNA is not only found in hair but also in the cytoplasm of every blood cell.

Just like the scene near the end of *The Wizard of Oz*, when Dorothy is told that she's always had the power she seeks—hers, in her ruby red slippers—I've had the greater part of my story on me at all times: my DNA history as told in my mitochondria and soon to be revealed in the sequencing of my gene by Professor Rees. Perhaps one really is the more important of our two tales—the dominant genetic trait to the recessive, mythic identifier that is our story. Both travel into us, like alleles, but one predominates. Genetics, which make all humans more than 99.9 percent the same, adds this tiny little twist, this identifier, these shadings we wear.

After Southport, I travel to Dublin by ship. I wanted to leave England from the Merseyside docks, like my grandfather, who came first, and my grandmother, who dragged her sewing machine the year after. Nodding at the sea, I think of the rigger whose deadly plunge into the brine must have been from right about where I am standing, right where the Victorian rigging lofts once clustered the harbor. Leaving the land behind, crossing the gangplank into the Seacat, my back is to the White Star Line building, still in Liverpool's skyline, from which Margaret Pilkington purchased her ticket on the *Teutonic*, the vessel that would take her to New York, to marry. The wake in which I am traveling is now my very own, that very specific genetic strain of red hair that emigrated exactly from here and went the distance into me.

*   *   *

Back at home, at my computer, I wait for the e-mail from Rees. After several weeks there should be a report on the sequencing of my gene. But it doesn't come and I note my exasperation, which, in turn, seems to make me want my marker more than ever, especially in light of the fact that here at home, I don't really appear to stand out as I once did. Maybe this notion of fading is getting to me. Here I am tracking the very thing I am losing by degrees.

As a child I had orange curly hair, so bright that it landed me on a poster for Kodachrome in the window of a Bell Boulevard photographer in Bayside, Queens. There I sat, in the bright sunlit window for all the world to see: a specimen of color almost running off the page. Blue overalls, holding a little gray clay dog, the crazy hazel eyes, a flounce of orange curls.

In college, my hair was the color of cherry varnish. One day, doing errands with a friend on Manhattan's Upper East Side, we stopped at the town house of a fashion photographer. Waving aside introductions, he took my hand and danced me into his studio, claiming I was his entry in a contest to discover the best original hair color. As he tipped unfiltered cigarettes from his lips to mine, his free hand ranged wildly through my long hair. It soon became an affair mostly to forget, but it left lasting images, including the name he gave my shade: "Red Hot Red." He won the contest, and the Clairol account.

And by the time my lover's father accused me of being many things, not one of them a redhead, it was only slightly more auburn. But now, even I have to admit that my own grip on this mantle is slipping.

We go gray for reasons unknown. Scientists have theories but no one actually understands the genetic purpose of graying. The most widely accepted version is infuriating: The fading of all hair color is a signal to the male of the species that women are passing their prime conception age, meaning that my original color reflected my childbearing potential.

While red hair does fade, it goes gray later than other colors, which, if the theory about childbearing is correct, would mean that even in a dimly lit redhead, this beacon still signals sex to the passerby. Perhaps if the bright red hair of youth is an indicator of fertility, this sheds some light on why we get so uncomfortable with bright bottle reds on elderly women. Maybe we are reacting to a defiant signal of sexuality long after society would have preferred that these women extinguish their notorious fire. Looked at purely in terms of its evolutionary advantage, beauty matters most for reproductive success. It's an asset that you use and are supposed to lose. Few of us, though, go willingly. Some of us refuse outright.

So while I was once redder than most—since only about 2 percent of the U.S. population comes by my color naturally—I am not as red as some and not nearly as red as I want to be. Which is how I found myself shortly after returning from the U.K., in the hands of the "Red Man of Manhattan," arguably the best red colorist in the trade.

"Blondes pay my rent," says John Fromer, rifling through my hair, "but reds are my specialty." He told me that he works up to changing a woman to red hair. And only with some women and only after knowing a woman for quite a while will he tell her that she'd make a good redhead. It's the personality that has to be there, he insists, and it should be "hot."

And at this statement, I am smiling. Until he drops a shank of my hair and says, "I wouldn't call it red. It's brown, highlighted red. We could add some blonde to deepen the red."

Eyeing Fromer, I know that if I am ever going to color it, it will be here with this man, whose life's work is tucked as close to the vest as anyone's I've ever seen, in little index cards lying in a pocket over his heart. One for each client. This is not one of those joints where there is one bottle for brown, one for red, and one for black. This is Kenneth (no apostrophe, please), the most posh salon in America, housed in New York's Waldorf Astoria hotel. It was here that owner Kenneth Battelle icon-ified the look of the twentieth century on the head of Jacqueline Kennedy, and here he still wields the shears.

"It's a little gray. It's faded," says Fromer, again with his hands in my hair. And then he whispers, "You could bounce this up at home."

Suggesting a product known in the trade as "color depositing" shampoo and conditioner, he sweeps away thousands of years, proposing an ancient product: madder, the dye found on the clothes of contemporary worshippers of Set, that old devil. Sold by companies like Aveda, it's considered a "natural" product meant for people who are not willing to go chemical but miss the color they know themselves to be. It won't cover gray, Fromer notes, but it will "bounce up" what was once red back to red.

And with it, I am back, fully red and wondering if this kind of product is part of the reason I see so many more redheads these days, that we have simply made it that much easier to be one—as well as stay one a little longer than before. Because there do seem to be many more red-haired women on the streets of America.

Clairol thinks so too. Red is at an all-time high. According to the hair care company, 30 percent of women between the ages of 18 and 34 who color their hair at home are going red; 27 percent are choosing brunette; 26 percent, blonde. The company also reports that sales of red at-home kits are rising steadily, with a 17 percent hike nationally after the turn of the recent millennium. Though they will not share exact figures, Goldman Sachs ascribes a number of $100 billion worldwide to the beauty industry, $38 billion of which is spent on hair care products alone. The industry is growing at 7 percent each year. Within that, for instance, L'Oreal, founded in 1909 and today's beauty industry elder, has experienced a compounded annual profit growth of 14 percent for more than ten years.

A big chunk of that revenue is spent on the advertising that thrums into us every day the notion that if you change your look, you can change your life. Which leads me to wonder just how the psychological paintings we have of ourselves have been rearranged to allow for any increase in red hair. If they are the same edits that allow for Lilith to be worshipped by feminists and worn in the hearts of contemporary pagans and witches, they are about reclaimed power. Powerful women can wear powerful color. When choosing red we are not choosing to be strumpets, harlots, hookers, liars, and witches, but rather to wear their totemic color, the shade of Mars as well as that of heartbreak, to see how we look. Whose hue is it? When we wear it, it becomes our very own.

But what are our choices these days? Having never colored my hair, trimming it only a few times a year and literally never having gotten a salon up-do, I have little sense of what's available; outside of the raw numbers, I am nearly naïve about what the beauty industry entails. That is, until I hit a trade show.

Like Italian opera and sitting up close in the movies, a trade show is a full-frame experience: loud, no distractions in the margins, nothing tangential, just pure unadulterated message that you cannot miss. And by the time I arrive at Manhattan's Jacob Javits Center, the International Beauty Show is just that: a throbbing mob of tout le monde de beauty. Of the four hundred exhibitors, maybe half are headset-miked, resulting in an aspic of sound bite promises of eternal youth that ricochet off the black walls and pierce the ears. The din is so thick that you might see it illuminated in a halo being created by the spray, lacquer, scrunch, and schvitz.

How did we ever get to this place? How did we, a renegade nation settled by plain-faced Puritans, get so quickly to hair extensions, nail extensions, and at-home hair color that lets us be anything we desire? In a word, *product*. What I have just walked into is an industry driven by the insistence of sex itself; sold, one product at a time, to as-yet-to-be-satisfied buyers.

What else could explain a woman in high-heeled, gold gladiator sandals strapped up her shins to her knees, sitting on the lip of a stage in front of thousands of people while she's getting her hair foiled? It speaks of the road to desire being paved with some pretty scary stops, including the sleeveless T-shirt on one redheaded hairstylist that reads, "I Run with Scissors." Nice.

The T-shirted stylist is lifting a shingle of the woman's dark brown hair to reveal that underneath is a peekaboo bright red patch. There are three guys in headsets on this stage alone. In turn they are teaching us—me and a mob of entranced stylists from all around America—to stand parallel, pinch hair, take scissors, lay on top, and snip all the way down, thus to take the weight out. He's making the model's head look like nothing so much as one of those carwash shammies that shimmies down onto your windshield in shaking shingles of cloth. The crowd goes wild.

Turning away, I see that it's everywhere: Hair is by far the biggest part of this show and all around the cavernous room there are individual stages and catwalks of men and women getting their hair poufed, moussed, and shorn. By the end of the three-day New York show, 47,000 people will have come through these doors.

In the statistic that best identifies the role of hair in contemporary society, a November 2004 piece in the *New York Times* reported that at Orlo, a Manhattan hair salon, clients are charged eight hundred dollars for a cut from hairdresser Orlando Pitta. It wasn't always like this. Hair was not always a hot topic. I remember the moment in time when blow dryers were big and black and something you went to the salon for, not something you had at home. Product had yet to be called product; mostly it was Prell, which was what your mother used. Hairdressers were older guys and part of your mother's marginal extended family, part confidante, part wizard; your father had a barber and the people who did your parents' hair had nothing in common except that they were both about to get left behind as stylists rocketed to sex-symbol status, becoming movie producers and bazillionaires, while Roberto's, the aquamarine place my mother and her mother attended once a week, managed little more than to twinkle in the reflected glow.

Worldwide, it is their daughters, the now fifty-something

women with fading hair color, who make up the largest segment of the coloring population. But right on their stiletto heels is the eighteen-to-twenty-five set—the mar-keted-to, overpolled, focus-grouped, money-burning-in-their-pockets young professionals—who have grown up entirely with the power to satisfy themselves at home. And in the little time it took for the grandmothers to beget the daughters to beget the granddaughters who are coloring their hair in record numbers, what also happened is that hair took back its sexuality and placed it in their eager hands. To them, hair has always been big.

Worldwide, the phenomenon of color has evolved into not just a fashion accessory, but also in reality, a personality accessory. The other demand of this generation, begun by their mothers, is to allow the woman coloring her hair to save time. To combine these goals into one and make them even easier to grasp, what is put in the hands of the consumer is an at-home product with a new name. What was once dye is now called color. Dyeing is for matching shoes to bags. Humans just don't dye any more. We color. And 60 percent of women who color their hair do so at home. To cater to them, companies like Revlon have even provided online hair color sites such as www.highdimen-sionhair.com, a place where clients can fill out a question-naire, view shade charts, and even e-mail the selected shade to a friend for consultation. At the end, the site visitor gets directed to a nearby retailer for purchasing the product.

And that's what I'm absorbing at the trade show, the stuff that you or I can buy anywhere. And in this throbbing billion-dollar, sexual world, the promise of ultimate desir-ability is placed in your very own hands; product lines like Bed Head come in hard plastic phallic-shaped dispensers that fit in your palm. Here, where the message is sex, redheads are not evil. They are an ideal. Counting again, I see numbers that rival Edinburgh. Redheads are everywhere. But here, instead of feeling like I am in a pack of me, I feel like something has been lost, something special. Something identifying.

The genotype, what alleles the organism has, depends on the phenotype, what it looks like, to ensure its selection and perpetuation, which, in turn, are heightened by the tale of red hair. But each of us, individually, establishes our own version, our identity. I was wrong in my conclusion before I went to the land of my ancestors. It's not that there are merely two traits that make up the identity of a red-haired person, two characteristics mirroring those two alleles. It's a threesome, the third being our own stories. The three are bound together like the strands of a braid: the genetics, the myth, and how we choose to live our personal tale. The idea comes to me as I try to apprentice to a rigger.

"Worm and parsle with the lay, turn and serve the other way," he says as we stand in the rigging loft at Mystic, Connecticut, the work appearing as laden with maxims as it is with metaphor. Hawser-laid rope is laid with the sun; cable-laid rope, against it. It is better to serve uphill, climbing rather than falling. Serving the rope is done with an apprentice who serves his time, serving the rigger who serves the rope, which may save their lives. I am learning to serve the rigger, Matt Otto, to whom I have come to lay my hands on the oldest piece of my tale.

A rope is strung tight between two points, stretching open the grooves between the turnings of the coils. We are filling in the grooves with spun yarn, filling the division between the strands, preparing it for serving, the apprentice holding the ball of spun yarn at some distance from the rigger, who turns the mallet, tightening the yarn into those grooves, pressing it down, stretching it into place, finishing the work.

Some time before he drowned in 1865, my great-great-grandfather had taken Mr. Dickens's 1860 advice that every man should get himself photographed. Years later, someone had shoved the slide into a cheap frame that lacked a dark backing, thus blotting out the image, and no one had seen it since. Vanishing from the glass, it simply left. But only for a while.

The week before visiting Mystic, I had taken the slide in its frame to a specialist in nearly extinct photographic techniques.

"Ambrotype," Michael Noonan had corrected me, taking it from my hand in his Saratoga Springs studio. A positive on glass, ambrotypes had a quick heyday for about a decade, starting in 1855, along with the albumen print, pretty much replacing the daguerreotype in popularity.

Getting it out of its frame was "going to be a bear," he asserted. We finally agreed that he should pry it with pliers. I squirmed as shards of glass showered from it like cracked ice. But the slide itself had adhered to the glass in the cheap frame. If we were unlucky, Noonan said, the image would be forever ruined when we pried them apart.

I went out into the parking lot to walk around. Well, I thought, I've got to do it. It's of no use to me the way it is. But I had come to treasure the little relic which had somehow survived since the 1860s, and which was inside now, possibly being lost forever. And with that thought I strode back into photographer's old-fashioned place of business, suddenly feeling the need to stop the whole thing, not willing to risk losing the slide entirely, however faint the image that remained.

"Got it," said Noonan, holding the bare glass slide in his hand just as I came through the door. The image was intact.

But after several unsuccessful attempts to back the slide with some dark fabric and view it, he finally suggested inserting it right into an old camera and shooting through it. Might burn the image right off, though.

Into the darkroom we went and he shot a few, then tossed what looked to me like a piece of bare paper into a huge tub of liquid, from which an antiquated system of armed baskets then lifted it and dropped it along in a series of baths, on to the next, then the next.

After ten minutes Noonan picked up the paper with tongs from its last basket and dropped it into a small tub. I stood over it as an image slowly assembled itself into place, coming back from the depths, bringing my genetic history into a watery focus, each line seeming to swim up through the liquid and directly into my soul.

"Oh my God," I said. It was a face I had seen so many times yet never seen, a face I missed so much: My grandfather's stare, my father's broad forehead, and then my cheekbones, all laid upon the florid face of what was undeniably a ruddy, red-haired man. All of it under a hat.

Having taken the photograph with me to Mystic, I had left it in its envelope, tucking it under my jacket. I was telling Matt Otto about it but hadn't yet brought it out. The last thing in the world I wanted to hear was that the man in the photo wasn't the rigger.

"A hat? Let me see it," Matt Otto said, urging me to get out the picture. I did.

Matt smiled.

"That's your rigger," he said.

His hands and face smudged with the black of the pine tar that only another rigger would recognize, Alexander holds his pose stiffly, a pose you see in photos like this, like Emily Dickinson's, those pictures that make us think of the Victorians as a miserable bunch, only to learn that this photo process required holding the pose for thirty seconds, so that no one in them smiled, no one moved, no one gestured for fear of the blur. Which makes it very unusual that Alexander is holding up a small cordial glass beside a decanter.

"I bet the rigging loft just got a big contract," said Otto.

"Maybe it was the birth of a child," I say, trying un-successfully to pull the tale back toward the topic of family.

"No, he's in his work clothes. His fall front slops. Not his Sunday clothes. And look at his hands."

I had looked at his hands countless times in the days since the photograph was made but could make no sense of the finger pads, spread farther than seemed possible until I served the line to Otto as apprentice.

"There was a district in Liverpool that made these," said Otto, tapping on the hat on the head of the rigger in the photograph. "That's all they did," said Otto.

"The hat?" I asked, amazed by his knowledge and how much I wanted this connection.

"It's straw. Called a broad-sennett hat. It's made of cane stock. Straw." Opening the *Ashley Book of Knots*, Otto showed me a flat braid that went into the hat on the head of my great-great-grandfather, the rigger, a red-haired Dane, taking me as far back as I can go to the people whose genes went forward from him through others and into my red-haired father, the mutation hurtling down both sides of my paternal line and running right into my red blood.

The tiny flat braid of the hat looks like the plaits in the hair of a woman long buried and the blur in my eyes makes everything look underwater. The action of the Mersey would have plunged the rigger's body down and hoisted it out to the Irish Sea atop one of the sediments of temperature, below the surface but above the silty bottom. His long hair, billowing down behind him, is freed now from beneath the straw hat of his hometown, the red locks minnowing down gently, fingering the small currents as the body is washed into the channel, burying him, finally, in the deepest part of my own story.

Over the holidays I went to a party at the home of my neighbors. I hadn't really wanted to go. It all just seemed so suburban, and when I had been dressing for it, I wondered if, home from my journeys, I simply appeared suburban, as well. But then we were there and within minutes I heard just the hint of a riff; the slightest whiff that somewhere there was music, real music, playing. I knew that my neighbor was in a band but to look at him I figured it was swing or something. I used to sing in rock and roll bands, but no one would know that to look at me now, married and mothering and tucked away behind a two-car garage.

In the next room were two men jamming, unplugged. Something stronger than my bad attitude got me into that room; something edging on idolatry of my youth made me ask, "Do you know 'Spider and the Fly'?"

The bald guitar player looked me up and down.

"Sit down," he growled. The song is an early sixties Mick Jagger vocal about a machine operator who says she likes the way he held the microphone. Serenaded by a middle-aged man in a neighborhood den, its lyrics rolled away my stone. And apparently I was not the only one.

Later that evening my husband sidled up to me at the buffet table.

"Honey," he said, sliding his arm around me. "There's a man in the other room who you've made very happy."

Apparently, after playing, the guitarist went to get a beer. He turned to a friend with a grin. "Great party, huh?" he said. "There's a chick with red hair in the other room who just asked me if I knew how to play 'Spider and the Fly.'"

A chick with red hair in the other room. Yes, there is.

Then, by Easter, an e-mail from Jonathan Rees.

Marion, Okay, here goes.

You have changes at codon 151 and 160. You are therefore homozygous for changes that we have previously shown to be associated with red hair and that we have shown in "in vitro" assays to show that the receptor shows diminished function.

You are therefore a typical red at least in terms of pigment genetics.

Yes I am.

Books

Witchcraft

Adler, Margot. *Drawing Down the Moon: Witches, Druids, Goddess Worshippers and Other Pagans in America Today*. New York: Penguin Compass, 1986.

de Givry, Grillot. *Witchcraft Magic & Alchemy*. Translated by J. Courtenay Locke. New York: Bonanza Books, no date.

Fisher, Amber Laine. *Philosophy of Wicca*. Toronto: ECW Press, 2002.

Hopman, Ellen Evert, and Lawrence Bond. *Being a Pagan: Druids, Wiccans and Witches Today*. Rochester, Vt.: Destiny Books, 2002.

Kramer, Heinrich, and James Sprenger. *The Malleus Maleficarum*. Trans. the Rev. Montague Summers. Mineola, N.Y.: Dover, 1971.

Paine, Lauran. *The Hierarchy of Hell*. New York: Hippocrene Books, Robert Hale & Co., 1972.

Robbins, Rossell Hope. *The Encyclopedia of Witchcraft and Demonology*. New York: Crown, 1959.

Seligman, Kurt. *Magic, Supernaturalism and Religion*. The Universal Library. New York: Grosset & Dunlap, 1968. Originally published as *The History of Magic*. Pantheon, 1948.

Valiente, Doreen. *An ABC of Witchcraft Past and Present*. New York: St. Martin's, 1973.

Art

Cooper, Suzanne Fagence. *The Victorian Woman*. London: V&A Publications, 2001.

des Cars, Laurence. *The Pre-Raphaelites: Romance and Realism*. London: Thames and Hudson, 2000.

Jiminez, Jill Berk, ed., and Joanna Banham, assoc. ed. *Dictionary of Artists' Models*. London: Fitzroy Dearborn, 2001.

Jolly, Penny Howell. *Made in God's Image? Eve and Adam in the Genesis Mosaics at San Marco, Venice*. Berkeley: University of California Press, 1997.

King, Ross. *Michelangelo & the Pope's Ceiling*. New York: Walker, 2003.

Mancoff, Debra N., and Jane Morris. *The Pre-Raphaelite Model of Beauty*. Rohnert Park, Cal.: Pomegranate Communications, 2000.

Marsh, Jan, and Pamela Gerrish Nunn. *Pre-Raphaelite Women Artists*. London: Thames and Hudson, 1998.

Mellinkoff, Ruth. *Outcasts: Signs of Otherness in Northern European Art of the Late Middle Ages*. California Studies in the History of Art, No. 32, Vol. 1. Berkeley: University of California Press, 1994.

Prose, Francine. *The Lives of the Muses: Nine Women & the Artists They Inspired*. New York: HarperCollins, 2002

Reynolds, Simon. *William Blake Richmond, An Artist's Life, 1842–1921*. Wilby, Norwich, England: Michael Russell, 1995.

Reynolds, Simon. *A Companion Guide to the Mosaics of St. Paul's Cathedral*. Produced for the Friends of St. Paul's Cathedral. Wilby, Norwich, England: Michael Russell, 1994.

Hair

Cooper, Wendy. *Hair*. New York: Stein and Day, 1971.

Jolly, Penny Howell. *Hair: Untangling a Social History*. With essays by Gerald M. Erchak, Amelia Rauser, Jeffrey O. Segrave, and Susan Walzer. Saratoga Springs, N.Y.: The Frances Young Tang Teaching Museum and Art Gallery at Skidmore College, 2004.

McCracken, Grant. *Big Hair*. Woodstock, N.Y.: Overlook, 1995.

Simon, Diane. *Hair: Public, Political, Extremely Personal*. New York: St. Martin's, 2000.

English Monarchy

Dudley, Donald R., and Graham Webster. *The Rebellion of Boudicca*. New York: Barnes & Noble, 1962.

Reid, Struan. *The Life and World of Boudicca*. Oxford: Heineman Library, 2002.

Weir, Alison. *Eleanor of Aquitaine: A Life*. New York: Ballantine, 1999.

Weir, Alison. *The Six Wives of Henry VIII*. New York: Ballantine, 1991.

Weir, Alison. *The Children of Henry VIII*. New York: Ballantine, 1996.

Weldon, Fay. "I, Boudicca." From *Nothing to Wear and Nowhere to Hide*. London: Flamingo/HarperCollins, 2002.

History, Myth, Story, Symbolism, and Taboo

Aristotle, *Minor Works*. Trans. W. S. Hett. Cambridge, Mass.: Harvard University Press, 2000.

Biedermann, Hans. *Dictionary of Symbolism*. Trans. James Hulbert. New York: Meridian-Penguin, 1994.

Bolen, Jean Shinoda, M.D., *Goddesses in Everywoman: A New Psychology of Women.* New York: Harper Colophon, 1984.

Brownmiller, Susan. *Femininity.* New York: Fawcett Columbine/Ballantine, 1984.

Bryson, Bill. *A Short History of Nearly Everything.* New York: Broadway, 2003.

Burton, Robert. *The Anatomy of Melancholy.* New York: New York Review Books, 2001.

Campbell, Joseph. *Myths to Live By.* New York: Bantam, 1973.

Davis-Kimball, Jeannine, Ph.D., with Mona Behan. *Warrior Women: An Archaeologist's Search for History's Hidden Heroines.* New York: Warner, 2002.

Dickens, Charles. *The Uncommercial Traveller.* New York: Books, Inc. Original copyright 1861.

Dickinson, Emily. *The Complete Poems of Emily Dickinson.* Ed. Thomas H. Johnson. Boston: Little, Brown. Twenty-first printing. Original copyright 1890.

Frazer, Sir James George. *The Golden Bough.* New York: Touchstone/Simon & Schuster, 1996.

Graves, Robert, and Raphael Patai. *Hebrew Myths: The Book of Genesis.* New York: Greenwich House/Crown, 1983.

Hamilton, Edith. *Mythology: Timeless Tales of Gods and Heroes.* Boston: Meridian/Little, Brown, 1969.

Hendrickson, Robert. *The Facts on File Encyclopedia of Word and Phrase Origins.* New York: Checkmark, 2000.

Ions, Veronica. *Egyptian Mythology.* London: Hamlyn, 1975.

Markale, Jean. *Women of the Celts.* Trans. A. Mygind, C. Hauch, and P. Henry. Rochester, Vt.: Inner Traditions, 1986.

Patai, Raphael. *The Hebrew Goddess.* Detroit: Wayne State University Press, 1990.

Pereira, Filomean Maria. *Lilith: The Edge of Forever.* Las Colinas, Tex.: Ide House, 1998.

Tannahill, Reay. *Sex in History.* Scarborough House, 1992.

Warner, Marina. *From the Beast to the Blonde: On Fairy Tales and Their Tellers.* New York: Farrar, Straus and Giroux, 1994.

Weitz, Rose. *Rapunzel's Daughters.* New York: Farrar, Straus and Giroux, 2004.

Wilson, A. N., *The Victorians.* New York: Norton, 2003.

Biblical studies

Avi-Yonah, Michael, and Emil G. Kraeling. *Our Living Bible.* New York: McGraw-Hill, 1962.

Kirsch, Jonathan. *The Harlot by the Side of the Road: Forbidden Tales of the Bible.* New York: Ballantine, 1997.

Metzger, Bruce M., and Michael D. Coogan, eds. *The Oxford Companion to the Bible.* New York: Oxford University Press, 1993.

Washburn College Bible. New York: Oxford University Press, 1979.

Etymology

Bartlett, John. *Familiar Quotations.* Boston: Little, Brown, 1968.

The Oxford Dictionary of Quotations. New York: Oxford University Press, 1980.

The Random House Dictionary of the English Language. Second Edition. New York: Random House, 1987.

Roget's International Thesaurus. New York: Thomas Y. Crowell, 1946.

Mice

Henwood, Chris. *Fancy Mice.* Neptune City, N.J.: TFH, 1995.

Young, Jack. *Mice as a Hobby.* Neptune City, N.J.: TFH, 1993.

Science

Ackerman, Jennifer. *Chance in the House of Fate: A Natural History of Heredity.* Boston: Mariner/Houghton Mifflin Co., 2001.

Browne, Janet. *Charles Darwin: The Power of Place.* New York: Knopf, 2002.

Gonick, Larry, and Mark Wheelis. *The Cartoon Guide to Genetics.* New York: Harper Perennial/HarperCollins, 1991.

Henig, Robin Marantz. *The Monk in the Garden: The Lost and Found Genius of Gregor Mendel, the Father of Genetics.* Boston: Mariner Books/Houghton Mifflin, 2001.

Keirsey, David, and Marilyn Bates. *Please Understand Me: Character and Temperament Types.* Del Mar, Cal.: Prometheus Nemesis, 1984.

Kevles, Daniel J. *In the Name of Eugenics: Genetics and the Uses of Human Heredity.* Cambridge, Mass.: Harvard University Press, 1997.

Pollan, Michael. *The Botany of Desire: A Plant's Eye View of the World.* New York: Random House, 2001.

Ridley, Matt. *Genome: The Autobiography of a Species.* London: Fourth Estate, 2000.

Starr, Douglas. *Blood: An Epic History of Medicine and Commerce.* New York: Knopf, 1998.

Sykes, Brian. *The Seven Daughters of Eve: The Science That Reveals Our Genetic Ancestry.* New York: Norton, 2001.

Understanding the Genome. By the Editors of *Scientific American.* Warner/Byron Preiss, 2002.

Watson, James. *DNA: The Secret of Life.* New York: Knopf, 2003.

Redheads

Ditz, Uwe, photographs, with text by Uwe Ditz, Barry Egan, and Irmela Hannover. *Redheads.* Zurich: Stemmle, 2000.

Douglas, Stephen. *The Redhead Encyclopedia.* Newport Beach, Cal.: StoneCastle, 1996.

Meyerowitz, Joel, text and photographs. *Redheads.* New York: Rizzoli International, 1991.

Literature

Aligheri, Dante. *The Divine Comedy.* Trans. Allen Mandelbaum. New York: Knopf, 1995.

Chapman, George. *Bussy D'Ambois.* Ed. Robert J. Lordi. Lincoln: University of Nebraska Press, 1964.

Chaucer, Geoffrey. *The Canterbury Tales.* Ed. J. U. Nicolson. Garden City, N.Y.: Garden City Books, 1934.

Dickens, Charles. *Great Expectations.* New York: Books Inc., no date.

Golding, William. *The Lord of the Flies.* New York: Putnam, 1954.

Heale, Elizabeth. *The Faerie Queene: A Reader's Guide.* Cambridge: Cambridge University Press, 1987.

Shakespeare, William. *The Complete Works.* The Pelican Text. London: Penguin, 1969.

Spenser, Edmund. *The Faerie Queene.* London: Penguin, 1987.

Wood, Michael. *Shakespeare.* New York: Basic/Perseus, 2003.

Rigging

Biddlecombe, Capt. George R. N. *The Art of Rigging.* Mineola, N.Y.: Dover, 1990.

Lever, Darcy. *The Young Sea Officer's Sheet Anchor.* Mineola, N.Y.: Dover, 1998.

From the Worldwide Press

Alexander, Hilary. "Moor the Merrier for Boudicca." *Daily Telegraph,* February 17, 2004. www.telegraph.co.uk

Alper, Joe. "Rethinking Neanderthals." *Smithsonian,* June, 2003.

"Britain's Prince Harry in Hair-Raising Mystery." www.cnn.com/world, December 14, 2002.

Carroll, Linda. "Gene for Red Hair May Help Suppress Pain in Women." *Reuters Health*, March 24, 2003. www.nlm.nih.gov/medline

Derbyshire, David. "The Genetics of Red Hair." *Daily Telegraph*, October 5, 2003. www.redandproud.com

Dixon, Cyril. "Should this Ad Make Gingers See Red?" *Daily Express*, April 19, 2000. www.express.co.uk

Dreifus, Claudia. "Shining a Light on the Health Benefits of Vitamin D." *New York Times*, January 28, 2003. www.nytimes.com

Garreau, Joel. "Red Alert! An Often Misunderstood Minority Finds It's Become a Mane Attraction." *Washington Post*, March 19, 2002.

"Gingerphobia: Carrot-tops see red." BBC News, E-Cyclopedia, March 22, 2000. www.news.bbc.co.uk

Gladwell, Malcolm. "True Colors: Hair Dye and the Hidden History of Postwar America." *New Yorker*, March 22, 1999.

Greenblatt, Stephen. "Shakespeare's Leap." *New York Times Magazine*, September 12, 2004.

Hechinger, John. "When a Judge Says 'Fat Tail,' Dapper Doesn't Turn a Hair." *Wall Street Journal*, May 17, 2002.

Henig, Robin Marantz. "The Genome in Black and White (and Gray)." *New York Times Magazine*, October 10, 2004.

Ingram, Sarah Sue. "Doll's Pregnancy a Shock to Some Shoppers." *Daily Press*, December 18, 2002. www.dailypress.com

Johnson, Marilyn. "Red Head Turners: A Favorite of Celebrities, Showstopping Shade Lends a Look of Unmistakable Drama." *Atlanta Journal-Constitution*, May 20, 2002. www.accessatlanta.com

Kimmelman, Michael. "The Eerie Exactness of the Daguerrotype." *New York Times*, September 26, 2003. www.nytimes.com

Kuczynski, Alex. "You Paid How Much for that Haircut?" *New York Times Magazine*, November 21, 2004.

Loyer, Michele. "Now it's Natural to Color Hair." *International Herald Tribune*, October 9, 1999. www.iht.com

Murphy, Rachel (Redhead). "Why Red is the New Blonde." *Daily Mirror*, August 3, 2004.

Neergaard, Lauran. "Are Redheads Harder to Knock Out Before Surgery?" *Associated Press*, October 14, 2002.

"One Strand of Killer's Hair and Detectives Get the Picture." Unbylined article. *Straits Times*, August 19, 2002.

Peterkin, Tom. "Scots May be Directly Descended from Neanderthal Man." *Scotland on Sunday*, April 15, 2001. www.aulis.com/news

"Pots of Promise." Unbylined article. *Economist*, May 22, 2003.

"Prince Harry 'honey trap' Allegations." BBC news Online, December 15, 2002, www.news.bbc.co.uk

"Red Hair Makes for a Fiery Temper, Judge Tells Defendant." Ananova, May 24, 2001. www.ananova.com

"Red Hair Raises Profile: Carrot Tops Claim They Have More Fun Than Blondes." *Cincinnati Enquirer*, May 14, 2002. www.enquirer.com

"Red Hair a Legacy of Neanderthal Man." *Sunday Mail* (Scotland), April 22, 2001.

"Redheads Are Neanderthals." South African Press Association, April 17, 2001. www.news24.com

Ridley, Matt. "What Makes You Who You Are." *Time*, May 25, 2003. www.time.com

Robinson, Anita. "Ginger Whinger and the Carrot Top Brigade." *Irish News*, November 15, 1999. www.irishnews.com

Rottenberg, Dan. "Do Redheads Have More Brains?" *Town and Country*, August, 1991.

"Scottish redheads 'more sexually attractive.'" Ananova, October 10, 2000, www.ananova.com

Smith, Dinitia. "Discovering Magdalene the Apostle, Not the Fallen Woman." *New York Times*, October 25, 2003.

Stanley, Alessandra. "Cleopatra, Career Woman." *New York Times*, January 20, 2001.

"Staying Sedated: While Blonds Have More Fun, Redheads May Feel More Pain." Unsigned article. *Health*, April, 2003.

Tan, Hwee Hwee. "A War of Words Over 'Singlish'." *Time*, Asia edition, July 29, 2002. www.time.com/asia

Van Biema, David. "Mary Magdalene: Saint or Sinner?" *Time*, August 11, 2003.

Wade, Nicholas. "Why Humans and Their Fur Parted Ways." *New York Times*, August 19, 2003.

Wade, Nicholas. "Geneticists Track More of Earliest Humans' First Itineraries." *New York Times*, November 12, 2002.

Wade, Nicholas. "Study Alters Time Line for the Splitting of Human Populations." *New York Times*, March 16, 1999.

Wade, Nicholas. "Y Chromosomes Sketch New Outline of British History." *New York Times*, May 27, 2003.

Wade, Nicholas. "Human Gene Total Falls Below 25,000." *New York Times*, October 21, 2004.

Wade, Nicholas. "Race-Based Medicine Continued . . ." *New York Times*, November 14, 2004.

Wade, Nicholas. "Similarities Found in Mouse Genes and Human's." *New York Times*, December 5, 2002.

"What is it about blondes?" BBC news online, March 28, 2001. www.news.bbc.co.uk

Wilford, John Noble. "Fully Assembled at Last, Neanderthal Stride Onstage." *New York Times*, December 31, 2002.

Young, Robin. "How Queen Boadicea Stayed on the Wagon." Times Online, February 19, 2002. www.timesonline.co.uk

Radio

Weldon, Fay. eBBC radio. "I, Boadicea." Read by Vanessa Redgrave. www.bbc.co.uk/radio4/discover/archive
Wright, Joe. "The Mother of All Lab Mice." *All Things Considered*, National Public Radio, September 18, 2002.

Journal Articles

Braun, Sidney D. "Lilith: Her Literary Portrait, Symbolism, and Significance." *Nineteenth Century French Studies*, University of Nebraska Press, Fall/Winter, 1982.

Clayson, D. E., and M. R. C. Maughan. "Redheads and Blonds: Stereotypic Images." *Psychological Reports*, 1986, vol. 59, 811–816.

Flanagan, Niamh, Eugene Healy, Amanda Ray, Sion Philips, Carole Todd, Ian J. Jackson, Mark A. Birch-Machin, and Jonathan L. Rees. "Pleiotropic effects of the melanocortin 1 receptor (MC1R) gene on human pigmentation." *Human Molecular Genetics*, 2000, vol. 9, no. 17, Oxford University Press, 2000.

Gevitz, Norman. "The Devil Hath Laughed at the Physicians: Witchcraft and Medical Practice in Seventeenth-Century New England." *Journal of the History of Medicine*, Oxford University Press, vol. 55, 2000, pages 5–36.

Ha, Tom, M.D , FRACP., and Jonathan L. Rees, FRCP., Fmed.Sci., "Melanocortin 1 receptor: What's Red Got To Do With It?" Edinburgh: *Journal of the American Academy of Dermatology*, December 2001.

Harding, Rosalind. "Genetic History of Modern Humans." Presented at the CEPH (Center for Polymorphism) Annual Conference, 2000.

Harding, Rosalind, Eugene Healy, Amanda J. Ray, Nichola S. Ellis, Niamh Flanagan, Carol Todd, Craig Dixon, Antti Sajantila, Ian J. Jackson, Mark A. Birch-Machin, and Jonathan L. Rees. "Evidence for Variable Selective Pressures at MC1R." *American Society of Human Genetics*, vol. 66, 2000.

Max, D. T. "Two Cheers for Darwin." *American Scholar*, Spring 2003, vol. 72, n. 2.

Mellinkoff, Ruth. "Judas's Red Hair and the Jews." *Journal of Jewish Art*, vol. 9, 1982.

Reed, T. E. "Red Hair Colour as a Genetical Character." *Annals of Eugenics*, 17:115–139, 1952.

Rees, J. L. "The Importance of Being Red." Dowling oration delivered at the Royal Society of Medicine, *Clinical and Experimental Dermatology* 24, 416–422, 1999.

Rees, Jonathan. "Complex Disease and the New Clinical Sciences." *Science*, April 26, 2002, vol. 296.

Rees, Jonathan L. "The Melanocortin 1 Receptor (MC1R): More Than Just Red Hair." *Pigment Cell Research*, vol. 13, 135–140, 2000.

Rees, J. L., and N. Flanagan. "Pigmentation, melanocortin and red hair." *QJM* 92, 125–131, 1999.

Rich, Melissa K., and Thomas F. Cash. "The American Image of Beauty: Media Representations of Hair Color for Four Decades." *Sex Roles*, vol. 29, 1993.

Seigworth, Gilbert R., M.D. "Bloodletting over the Centuries." *New York State Journal of Medicine*, December 1980, 2022–2028, Medical Society of the State of New York. From *Red Gold: The Epic Story of Blood*, a PBS production, with backup material provided online at www.pbs.org/wnet/redgold

Valverde, P., E. Healy, I. Jackson, J. L. Rees, and A. J. Thody. "Melanin pigmentation plays an essential role in protecting the skin from the damaging effects of ultraviolet radiation (UVR)." Paper presented for the Golden Melanocyte Award, 6th Meeting of the ESPCR, October 1995.

Internet Sites

All American Redheads, women's basketball team
www.allamericanredheads.com
www.wnba.com

Brenda Starr
www.comicspages.com/brenda

Dominatrix
www.ladylilith.com

Dryden, John
www.abebooks.com, source of a public-domain download of Eugene Field's "When Fanchonette Bewitched Me," in which the quote about Dryden's bookseller appears.

Eugenics
www.eugenicsarchive.org

Hair color at home
www.highdimensionhair.com

Mice
   American Fancy Rat and Mouse Association, www.afrma.org
   Clarke, Tom. "Mice make medical history." www.nature.com,
   December 5, 2002.
   www.rodentfancy.com
   www.miceandrats.com
Professor Jonathan Rees
   Professor Prefers Blondes, www.cpa.ed.ac.uk/bulletinarchive
Red Hair Genetics, www.derm.med.ed.ac.uk
Redheads
   www.realmofredheads.com
   www.gingernation.com
   www.redandproud.com
William Shakespeare
   Folger Shakespeare Library, www.folger.edu
Skin Cancer
   "Red Hair, Fair Skin, and Melanoma May be Linked to Variations
   of Same Gene."
   www.skincancer.org/redhair.php
Sperm bank
   www.cryobank.com

Sundry Publications

"Classifying Redheads—In the Interests of Science." Office of Com-
   munications and Public Affairs, University of Edinburgh, 2001.
"Emigrants to a New World." Brochure. Merseyside Maritime Mu-
   seum, National Museums and Galleries on Merseyside, Liverpool,
   England.
"Hair: Crowning Glory or Worst Nightmare." Mayo Clinic Women's
   HealthSource. March 2004.
"High Victorian Art." Brochure, National Museums and Galleries on
   Merseyside, Liverpool, England.
Overy, Caroline. "Charles Darwin: His Life, Journeys and Discov-
   eries." Catalog. English Heritage, 1997.
"Pre-Raphaelites." Catalog. Samuel and Mary R. Bancroft Collection
   of the Delaware Art Museum, 1995.
Prettejohn, Elizabeth. "Rossetti and His Circle." Catalog. Tate Gal-
   lery Publishing, 1997.
"Professor Prefers Blondes." Office of Communications and Public
   Affairs, University of Edinburgh, Bulletin 5, 2000–2001.
The Quill & Sword, Official Newsletter for the Witches' League for
   Public Awareness, Pagan Community Issue, vol. 4, no. 3.

"Red hair genes 100,000 years old." *Blueprint*, the newsletter of the University of Oxford, vol. 1, issue 11, May 31, 2001. www.ox .ac.uk

"Salem: Maritime Salem in the Age of Sail." Brochure. National Park Service, Division of Publications, for Salem Maritime National Historic Site, U.S. Department of the Interior, Washington, D.C., 1987.

Spencer-Longhurst, Paul. "The Blue Bower: Rossetti in the 1860s." Catalog. Barber Institute of Fine Arts, University of Birmingham, October 27, 2000–January 14, 2001. Sterling and Francine Clark Art Institute, Williamstown, Mass., February 11–May 6, 2001.

Whiteley, Jon. "Oxford and the Pre-Raphaelites." Catalog. Ashmolean Museum, Oxford University, 1993.

"Witches Yellow Pages, 2002–2003." Vol. 3, compiled by Gail Morrison and Julie Knapp.

A RECIPE

Lillian Hart Smith's Spam Chop Suey

Brown Spam in a little fat
Add:
2 chopped onions
1 cup chopped celery
1 can cream of chicken soup
1 can cream of mushroom soup
$1\frac{1}{2}$ cup water
$\frac{1}{2}$ cup uncooked rice
$\frac{1}{4}$ cup soy sauce
Bake, 1 hour, 350 degrees

ACKNOWLEDGMENTS

Many people contributed their unique scholarship and expertise to this book, but the synthesis of these ideas is my own, and I alone am responsible for the conclusions drawn in the braiding of this tale. I owe thanks to many.

Professor Jonathan Rees deserves credit not only for discovering the gene for red hair in humans, but also for seeing the story there waiting to be told. I hope I have done justice to both. Professional but humble, Professor Rees was a genuine good sport in giving me access to his lab and his vast knowledge. His assistant, Karen Muir, was instrumental in making my stay in Edinburgh quite lovely.

It was Kris Dahl who told me about Professor Rees, sitting me down one day in her office and presenting the idea like the gift that it was. She is a tenacious agent, but before that she is a marvelous friend, and I am so grateful. Jud Laghi, who assists her at ICM, treats us all with respect and lets us blow off the steam that sometimes builds in these pursuits.

Professor Ian Jackson in Edinburgh and Professor Rosalind Harding in Oxford were generous with their time, both at their offices as well as over the telephone, illuminating the complex science they each pursue.

Leila Meresman from the Wella Corp. was very helpful explaining the mesmerizing hair care industry, as was Nicole Martinez of One One Six Media, who enticed me to the beauty show, an unforgettable experience.

Dr. Kate Uraneck graciously introduced me to John Fromer, colorist extraordinaire at Kenneth Salon. John was kind enough to see me, share a few secrets, and run his hands through my hair.

Mary Zwolinski, folklorist and friend, sent out a mass e-mail to her colleagues, and back came piles of input. I am grateful to all who replied, but particularly to Ellen Damsky, Yvonne Milspaw, Jill Linzee, Ted McGraw, and Nicholas Burkaloff.

The Shakespeare people were tremendous in their support. Dr. Richard Kuhta, librarian at the Folger Shakespeare Library, and Elizabeth Walsh, head of research services at the Folger, explained things beautifully. Dr. A. R. Braunmuller, professor of English at UCLA, led me to myriad sources for folklore, superstition, and proverbs. Dr. Tom Berger, professor of English at St. Lawrence University, went line by line with me through passages of *As You Like It*, with his best tolerance.

Thanks to Dr. Harry Roy of Rensselaer Polytechnic Institute for giving me access to his genetics and evolution course. Dr. Dawn Starin was generous with her scholarship on menstruation.

At the American Philosophical Society in Philadelphia, Rob Cox was instrumental in arranging for me to view the eugenics files and for making me feel very welcome while doing so.

When it came to identifying and telling the story of the rigger Alexander Johnston, my great-great-grandfather, many people played a role. These included numerous sailing types, who straightened me out on what riggers do, what they wore, and how they lived. The first of these was Emma Tate, collection assistant at Stockport Heritage Services, in the Hat Works, who got me thinking about that hat on the head of the then-unknown man in the glass slide. After that,

Michael P. Dwyer, librarian at the Kendall Institute of the New Bedford Whaling Museum, informed me on the life of a rigger, as did Harry Hignett, vice president of the Liverpool Nautical Research Society. A lively group of Internet chatters on Spartalk at the Brion Toss Yacht Rigger site out of Port Townsend, Washington, debated various aspects of my search. Thanks also to Steve McGowan, a close friend and lifelong sailor, and Margaret Evans, assistant curator of Maritime Archives and Library at the National Maritime Museum in Liverpool. Those who were the greatest help were at Mystic Seaport, and include William Peterson, senior curator. At the Seaport's Henry B. duPont Preservation Shipyard, foreman Dean Seder was of immense assistance, as was lead rigger Matt Otto, who took me on as apprentice. I am forever grateful to Michael Noonan, a photographer in Saratoga Springs, for his remarkable artistry.

Graeme Marsden of the First Foot Guards of Massachusetts was wonderful on the topic of madder. The research of Cathy Mason of the New York State Historical Association on the Celts was a great help. Michael Oatman, artist and friend, graciously sat down with me over tea and talked about eugenics.

Explaining art is an art in itself. Dr. Penny Howell Jolly, professor of art history and Kenan professor of liberal arts at Skidmore College, was invaluable in her insight into iconography and hair and in directing me to the Skidmore College Library, a wonder in itself. She also led me to Dr. Ruth Mellinkoff, whose scholarship and insight made me look in places I would not have thought to look. It would be impossible to overestimate the value of Dr. Mellinkoff's understanding of Judas and his red hair as well as her ability to explain it to the reader. Steve Parissien, director of education at Sotheby's Institute of Art in London, led me to a greater understanding of the mosaics in St. Paul's, as did Jo Wisdom, librarian at the great cathedral. James Sturm, Vermonter, cartoonist, and director of the National Association of Comics Art Educators, was a great guide to sequential art, as was Herve St. Louis of Montreal. Dr. Margaretta S. Frederick, associate curator of the Bancroft Collection, Delaware Art Museum, picked me up at the train on her day off and showed me the Rossettis. Daria D'Arienzo, head of Archives and Special Collections at the Amherst College Library, could not have been more generous when showing me Emily Dickinson's hair and the daguerreotype.

Ronald Hutton, professor of history at the University of Bristol, helpfully shared his knowledge on ancient and medieval paganism.

Two of the kindest men in the world work in Lancashire, England. They are John Benson, of the Lancashire Records Office, who made a real effort and gave me the critical lead I needed, and Neville Green, warden of the Duke Street cemetery in Southport, England, who walked me to my family in the June rain.

Many people—on occasion, whole dinner parties—listened to my ideas, but it was Paul Ehmann who reminded me that you don't trip over the elephants, a crucial piece of advice at the time, and who made me laugh at myself. And on the subject of laughing, the experts are Bob Ludwig and Michael Ishizawa, our daughter's Brooklyn uncles and guides, in their own right terrific partners for more than a quarter century. For more than twenty years my friendship with Gary Taubes has benefited from me staying one book ahead (still am, Gar: keep writing). Jeanne Wein gave endless encouragement. Mary Elizabeth Orr went to witch camp with me, and I still can't believe it. She is the perfect pal—smart, brave, and able to whittle a wand on deadline. What else could a woman need in a friend?

Karen Rinaldi, head of Bloomsbury USA and redhead, said yes to the original proposal, and then did me the kindest of favors by putting me together with the person who gave me the greatest assistance of all—Gillian Blake, my editor at Bloomsbury. Gillian knows many things but perhaps foremost among them is how and when to say no. It's a needed skill, as well as a greatly underappreciated editing tool. Each time I went off in the wrong direction she was there, fists planted firmly on hips, guiding me back on track. I am more grateful than I can say here.

My family is my guide. Our daughter, Grace Yu Ying Smith, provides direction every day with her insistent curiosity, kind humor, and easy tolerance of all things. Every writer should ask a child's advice on where to get the energy for that next phone call. Grace never stops until her questions are answered. She is my hero. My sister, Margaret High Gun Roach, also provides me with a great work ethic as well as snappy comebacks to my worries. Richard Young listens and considers things—then, he speaks.

My greatest thanks is to Rex, my husband, who helped me pack, dropped me off, picked me up, read and reread and said yes over and over again. He is my one true companion, my love. Thank you.

INDEX

A NOTE ON THE TYPE

The text of this book is set in Linotype Sabon, named after the type founder Jacques Sabon. It was designed by Jan Tschichold and jointly developed by Linotype, Monotype, and Stempel, in response to a need for a typeface to be available in identical form for mechanical hot metal composition and hand composition using foundry type.

Tschichold based his design for Sabon roman on a font engraved by Garamond, and Sabon italic on a font by Granjon. It was first used in 1966 and has proved an enduring modern classic.